"The Julian Mystique makes a significan
covery in recent years of a remarkable
Feminine Divine in Christian tradition. In a style that is concise and
accessible to lay audiences, Frodo Okulam brings together a wide
array of biblical and historical sources to reveal the background of
Julian's theology of Motherhood.

"Another outstanding feature of this book is the connection
Okulam draws between Julian's age and our own, showing in both
the great need for the Divine Feminine. The questions for reflection
at the end of each chapter invite individuals and groups to expand-
ed spiritual insight and experience.

"In our ongoing journey toward a spirituality equally affirming of
women and men and of the goodness of all creation, Julian of
Norwich is a valuable companion. Through this excellent book,
Julian comes closer to us."

Jann Aldredge-Clanton
Author, *Praying with Christ-Sophia: Services for Healing and Renewal*
and *In Search of Christ Sophia:*
An Inclusive Christology for Liberating Christians

"This is a timely and important book. Like Thomas Merton of our
day, Julian of Norwich responds to our quest for grounding and
depth in these threatening moments at the end of the 20th century.
Julian assures us that 'all will be well.' Surely good news for our
time!"

Jim Conlon
Chairperson of Sophia Center, A Wisdom School Celebrating
Earth, Art, and Spirit
Author, *Earth Story, Sacred Story*

"The mystic Julian of Norwich, an outstanding figure among medieval women, is remembered chiefly for a paradox in her Revelations of Divine Love. Evil exists and evil there must be, yet 'all shall be well, and all shall be well, and all manner of thing shall be well.' That famous and haunting sentence is part of a rich record of visionary experience and reflection. Julian saw the mystery as resolved through God's love. For her, however, God was not a purely paternal deity. She discerned a feminine element in the Godhead, a divine motherhood.

"Such an idea might seem wildly original, even unorthodox. But Frodo Okulam's distinctive achievement is that she shows it to be rooted in scripture (notably the Wisdom literature) and in the language of some of the Fathers of the Church. Given this recognition, it becomes clear that Julian's insights can be powerfully relevant to Christian renewal at the present day."

Geoffrey Ashe
Author, *The Virgin*

THE
JULIAN
Mystique

Her Life and Teachings

FRODO OKULAM

TWENTY-THIRD PUBLICATIONS
Mystic, CT 06355

Dedication

To the memory of two fathers:
My father, Robert E. Lamoreaux

and to

Father Blaise Turck, OSB

and to

"our heavenly Mother...almighty,
all Wisdom, and all love." –Julian

Twenty-Third Publications
185 Willow Street
P.O. Box 180
Mystic, CT 06355
(860) 536-2611
800-321-0411

ISBN 0-89622-743-X
Library of Congress Catalog Card Number 97-60964
Printed in the U.S.A.

Acknowledgments

"We are all one in love."
–Chapter 9

This book is not only mine, but is the work of many who have helped me along the way. First of all, I want to thank Sally, Pat, and Jamie, who put up with my "reclusion" due to my research and writing, and provided well for the recluse. They helped me with 3:00 AM computer crises, did most of the housework, ran interference with phone calls, and provided encouragment and wisdom. My cat, Brian, provided humor and editorial help.

The Julian Mystique was born as a thesis for the Master's degree in theology at Mt. Angel Seminary. Sister Brigid Merriman, OSF, my thesis advisor, has been a great blessing to me. Her wise advice, humor, and spiritual example have made this project a joyous experience. She has continued to advise me throughout the publication process. I am also thankful to the late Father Blaise Turck, OSB, and to Sister Jane Ellen Burns, SNJM, for their suggestions.

The late Rev. Robert Pierce, of the Metropolitan Community Church (MCC), told me in 1989 I needed further education, preferably at a Catholic seminary, and my friend Sister Guadalupe Guajardo, SNJM, urged me to attend Mt. Angel. My mother, and posthumously my father, made this possible. The faculty, staff, and administration of Mt. Angel Seminary and the community of Mt. Angel Abbey were wonderful to me. The staff of Mt. Angel Abbey Library have been extremely helpful in providing references. Neil Kluepfel and Mary Carol Kendzia, my editors at Twenty-Third Publications, have helped me recast the thesis as a book.

My supervisor at Portland State University Library, Terry Rohe, allowed me to change my work hours to fit my school and writing schedule. I would also like to thank my student assistants at PSU, Sue Peltier and Sandie Grow, for their help.

Rev. B.J. "Beau" McDaniels has pastored me, and many in MCC have encouraged me in my studies. I am grateful to Rev. Lee Carlton for allowing me to interview him and include his beautiful vision in this book, and also to the founders of *WomanSpirit* magazine, Ruth and Jean Mountaingrove, for affirming my experience of the Goddess so many years ago.

Last, but definitely not least, I am deeply thankful to the women of SisterSpirit, my community. They have been patient with me, helping me and reaching out to help each other when I could not be there. They have taught me by example what sisterhood means.

Contents

Introduction

There is a great hunger in our times for positive female images of the divine. This longing can be found among both women and men of all traditions and beliefs. There is also a need among faith-filled people for a spirituality that is centering and universal, personally relevant, positive and affirming, accessible and balanced in its gender imagery.

Can this kind of spirituality, integrated and healing while affirming female imagery, be found within the Christian tradition? I believe so. It is in this context that the theology of Julian of Norwich—and in particular, her theology of motherhood—merits further examination.

The sources of information about Julian's personal life are few. She is mentioned in the wills of several people who were her contemporaries, as well as in the *Book of Margery Kempe,* but most of what we know comes from her own writings, the short and long texts which she called *Showings.* Ritamary Bradley, in an article titled "Julian on Prayer," writes "Julian...took care that we should know very little about her in order that we should not be distracted from the message she had to transmit."

Accordingly, the information she gives us is related to her visions. She tells us the exact date she received the revelations, transcribed in different manuscripts as either May 8 or May 13, in the year 1373. In both the short and long texts, she says the visions occurred when she was "thirty and a half years old," which places her birthdate sometime in November of 1342. At the beginning of the short text, the anonymous scribe (to whom the introductory paragraph is attributed) says Julian is "still alive, AD 1413." Three wills name her as a beneficiary: Roger Reed's will in March 1393, John Plumpton's in November 1415, and a third will of an unnamed donor in 1416. So we know Julian lived to be at least seventy-four years old, very old for medieval times.

Julian does not give us many more details about her life. We know much about her spirituality, her innermost feelings and reflections, and her theology, but little about her experiences except for the visions. At one point in the long text she says in passing that she has pondered the revelation and received "inward instruction" for "twenty years...except for three months," so we can estimate that she wrote the long text around February of 1393.

In this book, we will look at Julian's entire theology. But to do justice to her theology, we must first look at the context of her life. What was society like in Julian's times? What was the status of women in fourteenth-century England? These questions will be explored in the first few chapters, along with a study of the phenomenon of reclusion, the impact of the Black Death (bubonic plague) on Norwich, and an examination of what we know of Julian's life.

Following a brief discussion of textual considerations, we will then explore Julian's motherhood theology in detail. What was the precedent for such imagery? What does Julian make of this precedent? How did it affect the people of the times?

We will also look at the relevance of Julian's work for us today. We will discuss historical similarities between her times and ours, the need for her motherhood theology, and the work of people who exemplify this theological trend.

In writing this book, I have generally used the translation of Julian's *Showings* by Edmund Colledge and James Walsh (*Julian of Norwich: Showings,* Classics of Western Spirituality series, Paulist Press, 1978). This translation contains both the short text and the long text, and is based on the critical edition by the same scholars. Direct quotes from the *Showings* are referenced to chapters in either the short text (Roman numerals) or the long text (Arabic numerals).

By looking at Julian's work in its own context and in relation to our times, we can arrive at a deeper understanding of the theology and spirituality of Julian of Norwich, with insights relevant to our spiritual needs today.

Julian Chronology

November 1342	Julian is born.
May 1349	Plague reaches Norwich. Forty to forty-five percent of the population dies. Julian is seven.
1361–2	Second wave of plague. Twenty percent of the population dies. Julian is nineteen.
1369	Third wave of plague. Thirteen percent of the population dies. Julian is twenty-seven.
May 8 (13), 1373	Julian's visions. She is "thirty and a half years old."
May 9 (14), 1373	Julian's sixteenth revelation.
?	Julian writes the Short Text
1375–1390	Recurrences of the Black Death
February 1393	Julian writes the long text "after receiving inward instruction for twenty years, except for three months." Julian is fifty.
March 1393	Roger Reed's will names Julian a beneficiary. Julian is in the anchorhold.
1412 (or 1413)	Margery Kempe visits Julian. Margery is thirty-nine; Julian seventy.
1413	Julian "still alive" according to the heading of the short text MS.
November 1415	John Plumpton's will benefits Julian.
1416	Last bequest to Julian, who is now seventy-four.

CHAPTER ONE

Women in the Middle Ages

What was it like for Julian, growing up as a woman in the Middle Ages? Conditions in early medieval society (approximately 850 AD to 1050 AD) had not been conducive to women's freedom. The culture was oriented toward warfare, and women were separated by rigid class boundaries. Primogeniture, the practice of inheritance by birth order, meant that even aristocratic women might not achieve independent status. Attitudes toward women either placed them on a pedestal as virgin or denigrated them as temptress. Religious convents were open to the upper class only, and class determined status within the religious community. The legal status of women was on a par with that of children: they were recognized but not allowed to administrate.

In the late eleventh and early twelfth century this situation began to change as the population became increasingly urbanized. Townspeople were not subject to the same feudal system which governed earlier agricultural communities. Advancing technology in the crafts provided opportunities for female labor in the trades. Women became members of trade associations and acquired a new legal status as property owners. The population of Western Europe became increasingly female due to male deaths in battle and absence on various Crusades, the first of which was mounted in the year 1095.

In an article titled "The Anchoress in the Twelfth and Thirteenth Centuries," Patricia Rosof writes:

> By the twelfth century, towns and cities were springing up throughout Europe. By this time, too, women had come to outnumber men, particularly in these cities. At the same time these towns, with their majority female populations, were developing new religious sentiments and movements began appearing.

In the mid-eleventh century, the Gregorian Reform consolidated ecclesiastical power in the hands of the clergy, ordering a reform of life for wayward priests and emphasizing the eucharist under priestly authority. The clergy were radically set apart from both the laity and the political structures of Europe, and a clear hierarchy developed within the order of priesthood.

Both this reform and the increasing shift of the population to urban centers gave rise to a renewal within monasticism since it had grown more remote from the needs and experiences of the laity. The old monastic goal of withdrawal from the world through renunciation of family and private property had become inadequate, as upper-class monks and nuns remained part of a wealthy collective. There grew, however, a new religious poverty movement which renounced landed wealth—even collective wealth—as well as the newfound urban prosperity. Some groups withdrew from society, living in the wilderness and surviving by means of their own hands, while others sought to live the apostolic life by preaching the Gospel among the people.

This search for the *vita apostolica* in the twelfth and thirteenth centuries appealed to both women and men. Women especially joined both old and new religious orders in unprecedented numbers. Perhaps even more than men, women fled the rigid roles forced on them by their families and insisted on choosing their own path in life. The mood of the times among the orders toward renouncing family wealth accorded with these desires.

At first, the church hierarchy approved of the movement of women into religious communities as a way to prevent them from falling into the heretical sects, who also were enthusiastically welcoming women. Eventually, however, the hierarchy became more and more nervous about both the flood of women into religious orders and the creation of new orders in general. This anxiety culminated in the issuance of a decree by Fourth Lateran Council in 1215 forbidding the creation of new religious orders. The male religious also grew increasingly dismayed at the flood of women into their ranks. In 1228, the Cistercians issued an order forbidding all further attachment of nunneries, and the Premonstratensians (a religious order founded in 1120 by Norbert of Xantan), disavowed any responsibility for their nuns.

As the monastic orders closed ranks against them, women moved toward the secular religious poverty movements. Some joined the Poor Clares, founded by St. Clare and St. Francis in 1212, and others the movement known as the

Beguines. The Beguine movement arose in the urban centers of Europe, among women of all social classes. The openness of this way of life to all women was unprecedented. Not an organized monastic order but a grass-roots spiritual movement, the Beguines vowed chastity and to live by manual service. They might live alone or among others in a beguinage. In any case, these women, whether Beguines or Poor Clares, wished not only to be poor but to live with the poor.

It is possible that Julian was a Beguine in her youth. Although there is no positive evidence of this, Julian's emphasis on her fellow Christians suggests identification with the laity, perhaps in a lay order such as the Beguines.

Questions for Reflection and Discussion

1. Julian said she received "inward instruction" for twenty years. Have you ever had an experience of this kind? Did you share what you received with anyone else?

2. Women fled the rigid roles forced on them by their families in the twelfth and thirteenth centuries, and insisted on choosing their own path in life. Can you relate to this? What does it feel like?

3. What was the reaction of the medieval male religious hierarchy to the flood of women into monastic orders? How might this parallel the movement of women today into more ministerial roles within the church?

4. In the twelfth and thirteenth centuries, the religious poverty movement renewed monasticism. Are we in need of spiritual renewal today? What form might this take? Do you see any similarities between the medieval grass-roots spirituality of the Beguines and any contemporary spirituality movements?

5. One of the goals of the Beguines and of the Poor Clares was "not only to be poor but to live with the poor." What is the difference between being poor and living with the poor? Can you give contemporary examples? How would it affect your current life-style if you were to adopt this goal?

CHAPTER TWO

Julian,
Anchoress

One of the roots of Beguine spirituality was the tradition of the desert Fathers and Mothers. This tradition was characterized by asceticism, feats of physical endurance, interior silence, compassion, and humility.

The purest form of the desert experience was the solitary life, and the recluse embodied this ideal. Ann K. Warren, in her book *Anchorites and their Patrons in Medieval England*, says,

> By a process of internalization, both the physical martyrdom of the earliest Christian centuries and the search for the desert that had followed in its wake...became mental states. What had been actual became symbol-

ic....the medieval anchorite's refuge...drew the recluse
back in time to the desert caves of the Egyptian saints.

The words "anchorite" and "hermit" reflect this tradition.
Hermit is derived from the Greek word for desert, *eremus,* and
anchorite from the Greek *anachorein,* to withdraw. While hermit retained its general usage, anchorite came to refer to one
who chose to be enclosed.

We know that Julian was an anchoress (a female anchorite)
from the preface to the short text, the wills which named her
as a beneficiary, and the writings of Margery Kempe,
although we don't know when she actually became an
anchoress. It is possible that she was already enclosed at the
time of her vision, but Julian's mention of the presence of her
mother (Chapter x) and of the parish priest accompanied by
a child at her bedside (Chapter vii) may argue against this.
The first evidence we have of her being an anchoress is in
Roger Reed's will of 1393, so it is possible she was not
enclosed when she wrote the long text. The deep reflection
and the scholarship found in the long text, however, lend cre-
dence to her having been an anchoress during the intervening
years.

Julian's education has been a matter of diverse opinion
among scholars. Some have accepted at face value her protes-
tations of ignorance. Others, such as Edmund Colledge and
James Walsh, have posited that she not only knew the Latin
Vulgate Bible, but was familiar with the writings of Augustine,
Gregory the Great, William of St. Thierry, and contemporary
works like *The Cloud of Unknowing* and Chaucer's *Boethius,* as
well as being an accomplished rhetorician.

In the *Showings,* Julian says she is not a teacher, "but a
woman, ignorant, weak, and frail" (Chapter vii). In the long
text she says the revelation was made to a "simple, unlettered

creature" (Chapter 2). Although it would be plausible for an illiterate woman to compose works through dictation, Grace M. Jantzen, in *Julian of Norwich: Mystic and Theologian,* points out that her careful literary organization and cross references within the texts make this unlikely. We know that she could not have received a formal university education, as that was closed to women in her day. Colledge and Walsh are convinced she became a nun in her teens, and received her education in the convent. Perhaps she was not a nun, but attended Carrow Abbey boarding school, which would have been open to her if she was upper class or wealthy. She could also have been self-taught; this was a possibility for a woman of her intelligence who had access to a library, and there was an excellent library at the Augustinian friars' house across the street from St. Julian's Church in Norwich.

Based on her writing alone, it seems clear that Julian was able to read and write in the vernacular, and that she had read the Latin Vulgate Bible and other spiritual texts. Colledge and Walsh call her book "a great monument to the…traditions of *lectio divina…*the loving, prayerful study and memorization of sacred scripture." Julian undoubtedly employed this method and was a learned woman, wherever she received her education.

Why, then, does she say she is unlettered? Certainly she is humble, and her humility is especially refreshing compared with the self-aggrandizement of her contemporary, Margery Kempe. But she is not just practicing humility as a pious virtue. In the short text, Julian writes:

I am not good because of the revelations, but only if I love God better.…For I am sure that there are very many who have never had revelations or visions, but only the common teaching of Holy Church, who love

God better than I. If I pay special attention to myself, I am nothing at all, but in general I am in the unity of love with all my fellow Christians (Chapter vi).

Julian does not emphasize her education because she believes it is love of God that is good. She commends those who have "only the common teaching of Holy Church" and also those who contemplate Jesus, who is everyone's teacher. No doubt many praised Julian for her knowledge, but it was not this kind of glory Julian desired. Julian would say with Paul, "May I never boast of anything except the cross of our Lord Jesus Christ" (Galatians 6:14).

Julian tells us that in the vision Christ says to her, "I thank you for your service and your labour, and especially in your youth" (Chapter viii). What was this service? Was Julian a nun before entering the anchorhold? Many recluses began religious life in a monastery. Since the Benedictines served St. Julian's Church, it is possible she was a member of that community before taking up her new vocation as an anchorite. But there is no mention of monastic practice in her book. As Grace Jantzen puts it, "It simply does not breathe the air of a convent."

Jantzen thinks it is possible Julian was a Beguine before entering the anchorhold. Her spirituality does share a common focus with the Beguines, whose mystical piety was Christocentric and concerned with sharing the sufferings of Christ. Or perhaps she was of independent means. She does not mention a major benefactor, though later in her life she does receive benefices. Whatever her service was in her youth, Julian retained a desire to serve Christ more fully, and followed that calling to the anchorhold by the time she entered her fifties.

The Life of a Recluse

Why did people desire to become recluses? According to Aelred of Rievaulx, a noted twelfth-century Cistercian abbot, there were three reasons for becoming a recluse: to escape the dangers of life in society, to avoid its troubles, or to adhere more closely to Christ. Although both practical and spiritual motives led women to seek enclosure as anchoresses, the primary reason was usually spiritual. Some were nuns who had lived for a time in a convent and desired a stricter life, and the solitary path was considered to be more difficult than monastic life, closer to its desert roots and the contemplative ideal. St. Benedict saw the anchorites as "fighting against the devil...in single-handed combat...God alone aiding them."

Women who chose this life were generally strong, highly motivated women. They often were under parental pressure to marry or to continue in the less rigorous monastic community. Before being allowed to live as an anchoress, they underwent extensive testing of their call. Their longing to draw closer to God strengthened them through these trials.

Anchorites sought to draw close to God through contemplation, and the penitential aspects of the reclusive life were seen as preparation for the spiritual journey. Julian's visions of Christ on the cross recorded in the *Showings* were a form of a common contemplative technique of the time, where one would try to develop a sense of being present at events in the life of Christ.

There were practical reasons, too, as Aelred said, for reclusion. According to Margaret Wade Labarge in *A Small Sound of the Trumpet: Women in Medieval Life*, "recluse" was listed under "trades and occupations" in Henry III's Liberate Rolls. This "trade" was open to women of all social and economic backgrounds, as monasteries at this time were not. The church anchoress position provided a practical life-style for increasing numbers of urban women. No dowry was required upon entry into reclusion, as it was in nunneries, but the prospective anchoress had to show that her maintenance had been arranged. If she was wealthy she could endow herself, but if not she could find patrons or partially support herself through needlepoint. Patrons might be wealthy individuals, such as kings or bishops, or a monastic community if the cell was attached to a monastery. In cases where the anchoress received more than she needed she would recirculate gifts back to the church and to the poor.

The bishop of the diocese in which the recluse was to reside was responsible for screening candidates, arranging the rites of enclosure, and providing ongoing spiritual direction. Once the permission of the bishop was obtained, the bishop or his representative performed the rites of enclosure. These rites might include a Mass of the Holy Spirit as well as prayers from the Office of the Dead. The death-imagery served to reinforce the recluse's renunciation of earthly fulfillment. The ceremony ended with the symbolic blocking of the door and an antiphon: "Here is my resting place forever."

The cell which the anchoress entered upon enclosure was a small house attached to a church, chapel, hospital, or monastery. Usually it had two rooms, a bedroom and a parlor, and two windows, one looking into the church and one toward the outside. Through the church window the recluse could follow Mass or receive communion. The outside window was covered with a curtain so that the anchoress's face remained hidden, but her voice could be heard. Some anchorholds had gardens or courtyards attached.

We do not know what Julian's name was before she entered the anchorhold. It was the custom for an anchoress to adopt as her own the name of the church to which she was attached. Since Julian's cell was attached to the parish church of St.

Julian, this is how she became known. We also do not know which St. Julian the church was named for, although Grace Jantzen speculates it may have been St. Julian the Hospitaller, patron saint of ferrymen, because there was a ferry crossing near the church.

Julian would not have been without companionship in her everyday life. An anchoress was attended by one or two servants, who cared for her domestic needs. In *A Rule of Life for a Recluse*, written for his sister, Aelred recommends an "elderly woman" and a "strong girl capable of heavy work." The *Ancrene Riwle*, which was a thirteenth-century guide for anchoresses also known as the *Ancrene Wisse,* allows a recluse to keep a cat. Although we do not know whether she indeed had a cat, iconographer Robert Lentz depicts her with one in a recent icon of Julian. There is also an illuminated cat in the window of the modern St. Julian's Church in Norwich, England. In his article "Solitude and Solidarity: Medieval Women Recluses," Jean Leclercq likens the relationship between the recluse and animals to that of Christ in the wilderness, dwelling with the beasts.

The daily life of the anchoress was not regimented by monastic routine. She followed a quasi-monastic schedule, with time for silence as well as time for speaking to her servants and with visitors. Living alone, the anchoress could decide her own hours of prayer, work, meditation, and spiritual direction. Her clothing was practical, and her food simple. All the activities and particulars in an anchoress's life were patterned to allow time for contemplation of the divine.

An anchoress's cell was designed to serve her devotions. The cross, an altar, the image of the Virgin and one other saint served to focus her prayers, while the window into the church encouraged devotion to the Eucharist. Patricia Rosof writes:

The singularity of the life, the fact that recluses were encouraged to find the best spiritual mix for themselves, to favor short meaningful prayers over long, drawn-out ones, all encouraged mystical, interior experiences.

Rosof further calls the experience of visions "the preaching medium of the anchoress." Through the visions received in their private devotions, anchoresses gave direction to those who sought their advice and contributed to the spiritual life and theology of the larger community.

The status of the recluse in the community was high. In towns, the presence of the anchoress served to remind people that someone was praying for them. Townspeople felt pride in their recluse, knowing she was lifting them up in prayer. Jean Leclercq beautifully describes the relationship of the contemplative to the community: "The monastic person is one who is centered in such a way that in this one person converge as in a single focal point the centers of every other reality." Anchoresses in the High Middle Ages (approximately 1150 AD to 1350 AD) served as this focal point, and Julian is central among them, voicing so well the spiritual and theological vision of her day.

Margery Kempe and Julian

There is an account of Julian's spiritual counseling given by her contemporary, Margery Kempe, also a mystic, whose *Book* is the only other known writing by an Englishwoman during Julian's time. Margery was born around 1373 and visited Julian in 1412 or 1413, when Margery was thirty-nine and Julian seventy. In the Introduction to her edition of *The Book of Margery Kempe,* Hope Emily Allen says Margery and Julian were "as unlike as two human beings can be." Other commentators refer to Margery as self-preoccupied, exactly the opposite of Julian, and this can easily be seen in her book.

Margery was illiterate, so her book is dictated. She does not mention Julian's book, and it is likely she did not know it. Yet her report of Julian's words strikes one as extremely accurate, reproducing Julian's philosophy and even her turns of phrase, such as "for he is all love [charity]." Margery's personality comes through in this report—she is at pains to extol her own virtues and emphasizes the "many days" that she was with Julian.

Margery is bidden by God to go to Julian to ask her if there is any deceit in her own revelations, for "the anchoress was an expert in such things and could give good counsel." Margery's account continues:

> The anchoress, hearing the marvelous goodness of our Lord, highly thanked God with all her heart for his visitation, counseling this creature to be obedient to the will of our Lord God and fulfill with all her might whatever he put in her soul if it were not against the worship of God and profit of her even-Christians, for, if it were, then it were not the moving of a good spirit but rather of an evil spirit. The Holy Ghost moveth never a thing against charity, and, if he did, he were contrary to his own self, for he is all charity.

Julian saw through Margery's self-importance, counseling her to forbear the world's judgment with patience and trust in God:

> Setteth all your trust in God and feareth not the language of the world, for the more despite, shame, and reproof that you have in the world the more is your merit in the sight of God. Patience is necessary unto you, for in that shall you keep your soul.

From advice such as this we can see that Julian was a wise counselor, that her theology informed her counseling, and that she was a good judge of character. Margery's respect for her is evident. In fact, she says in the very next sentence after concluding the account of her visit to Julian that she has visited "many a worthy clerk, worshipful doctors of divinity, both religious men and others of secular habit." We will see how fitting the respect of her contemporaries was when we look further at Julian's theology.

Questions for Reflection and Discussion

1. Have you ever experienced periods of solitude or silent retreat? How did you feel? Did you gain spiritually from the experience? If you have not had these experiences, would you like to? Why or why not?

2. Both the Beguines and Julian share a piety centered on the sufferings of Christ. Why do you think people practice this form of piety? Have you ever practiced this type of devotion? Was it a positive or negative experience for you?

3. During the enclosure ceremony, the anchoress left her former life and name behind forever. Have you experienced a similar rite of passage? Was it marked by a ceremony? If you have not experienced this, what do you think it would be like to leave the world, or a former way of life, completely behind?

4. Have you ever had mystical, interior experiences? What were they? What subsequent effect did they have on your life?

5. What place, if any, has spiritual direction held in your life? Is there someone you have gone to for "good counsel" as Margery did to Julian?

CHAPTER THREE

Norwich and the Plague

During the late Middle Ages, Norwich was a popular trade center with especially strong ties to Germany and the Low Countries. It was located northeast of London, in the county of Norfolk, found in a section of England known as East Anglia. The town had about 10,000-12,000 inhabitants during Julian's day, and was at that time the second or third largest city in England.

Norwich lay on the River Wensum, a navigable river, almost at the point where the Wensum converged with the River Yare, which flowed into the North Sea. The Hundred Years War between France and England had begun in 1337, and this conflict increased the danger of piracy to England's southern ports for the ensuing century. Therefore, the more northerly trade centers, including Norwich, took on greater importance in the commerce of the late Middle Ages.

There was a higher proportion of recluses in the county of Norfolk than anywhere else in England during the fourteenth century, although this cannot be attributed to any one thing in particular. A major house of Beguines was located there and a Benedictine convent, as well as houses of all the major orders. The Benedictine cathedral priory was an important center of learning for the area. There were many churches constructed in Norwich during the twelfth through fourteenth centuries, some thirty of which are still standing. (St. Julian's Church was reconstructed after being bombed in 1942).

When Julian was a girl of seven, the Black Death (bubonic plague) hit Norwich for the first time. The plague had originated in the Far East, and by 1346 was identified in the Crimean port of Kaffa, located on the Black Sea near present-day Ukraine. Borne by fleas that lived on rats, the plague traveled with the rats in the holds of Italian merchant ships. In 1347, the plague was found in Byzantium, Rhodes, Cyprus, and Sicily, and by winter of 1348 it was in Venice, Genoa, Provence, and Marseilles. It spread northward during 1348, reaching Weymouth, England, in August of 1348 and Norfolk in May of 1349.

The disease came in three forms: bubonic, pneumonic, and septicaemic. The bubonic strain brought swellings at the point of the flea bite, swollen lymph nodes, and purplish blotches *(buboes)*. The deadlier pneumonic strain, which was also more contagious, brought coughing and vomiting of blood. The septicaemic form entered the bloodstream directly and death might occur before any symptoms appeared.

During the first wave of the plague in Europe, an estimated thirty percent of the population died. In England, the percentage was the same or higher. The plague took the deadly pneumonic form in Norwich, where its effect was intensified by the cool northern weather, and an estimated forty to forty-five percent of the population died. Among the clergy, the impact was even greater, and about half of them died. The second wave, in 1361–62, when Julian was nineteen, killed twenty percent of the remaining population in England. The third epidemic struck in 1369, Julian's twenty-seventh year, taking thirteen percent of the people.

Was 1373, the year of Julian's visions, a plague year? Could the illness that led to her visions have been plague? Julian does not say her illness was plague, nor does she mention plague symptoms, and I think if it were plague there would not have been a child present at her bedside (Chapter vii). In any case, the impact of the Black Death on Julian's life would have been very great. Plague outbreaks recurred in 1375 (two years after Julian's visions), in 1379, 1383, 1387, 1390, and 1399-1400, and at intervals throughout her remaining years.

The plague, with its sudden onset and swift death, high mortality and frequent recurrences, set the whole society of medieval Europe into crisis. In the initial shock of the first wave of illness, everyday life ceased. People deserted their trades and their kin—parents abandoned children and lovers one another, leaving them to die alone. Even the clergy stopped giving last rites.

In the face of death, many tended toward hedonistic excess in which traditional values and practices were abandoned. The recurrences of the epidemic heightened feelings of pre-cariousness, helplessness, and alienation from former social norms. At the same time, some people clung more strongly to tradition, while others, seeking certainty in the face of uncertainty, became more fundamentalist. Many of the older aristocratic families emphasized chivalry as a way of winning favor with God and warding off the plague.

Persecutions escalated, focusing particularly on massacres of Jews and witch-burnings. In 1374, Pope Gregory announced the right of the Inquisition to intervene in sorcery trials, which previously had been a civil matter, thus launching the involvement of the church in the witchcraft persecutions. People were fascinated with death and with the most terrifying aspects of pain, which was reflected in post-plague art and literature.

Many took the Black Death to be an eschatological sign and called for repentance. Plague-induced penitence could take extreme forms, such as self-flagellation. Julian herself, having outlived most of the people she knew (based on mortality estimates for Norwich), prayed for an illness so she could serve God better. Piety, too, changed in the face of this crisis in faith. It became more external and spectacular, while the Christology of the time emphasized the miraculous and supernatural. Many sought salvation through increased good works, including charity and pilgrimages. There was a widespread interest in mysticism and lay piety, noted by Robert S. Gottfried in his book *The Black Death: Natural and Human Disaster in Medieval Europe:*

> While confidence in the institutional church waned, faith in Christianity itself did not; rather the imminence of death, brought closer than ever by plague, made the need for salvation more pressing. One consequence was the spread of mysticism and lay piety....Aside from their most profound sincerity, the most striking characteristic of mysticism and lay piety was the lack of need for a formal clergy to lead the way to paradise. Many post-plague Christians felt they could communicate directly with God.

In terms of the loss of human life, the Black Death has been called the second worst disaster in history, outranked only by World War II. Others have said that because of the changes which the plague wrought in society, it should be considered the greatest disaster ever to strike the human race in historic times. England's mortality was worst of any of the countries of Western Europe, and the impact on Norwich was the greatest in England.

Yet amid one of the greatest disasters ever known, Julian comes, a light of hope within the storm.

Questions for Reflection and Discussion

1. Can you imagine what it was like to live through the plague? Describe how you might feel if you were living then. Can you name any present-day parallels? Discuss similarities and differences between now and then.

2. Why do you think the plague led to persecutions? Do these conditions exist today? What could help stop such persecutions?

3. Have you ever experienced a crisis in faith? What led to this? What did you do about it? If you have not experienced this, have you helped others with such a crisis? What did you do?

4. Where do you observe extreme penitence or extreme hedonism in today's world? What are some possible reasons for these two types of behavior?

5. Have you ever been through a disaster or a life-threatening situation? Did you have any mystical experiences associated with this? If not, what have you heard others say about these situations?

CHAPTER FOUR

The Showings

Julian's revelations began early in the morning, about 4:00 AM, and lasted through fifteen revelations until 3:00 PM of that day. The sixteenth revelation was shown her on the following night. She received the revelations in three ways: "by bodily vision, and by words formed in [her] understanding and by spiritual vision" (Chapter 73).

The revelations come in answer to prayer. From her youth, Julian prayed for three gifts of God. These are set forth in Chapter 2 of the long text. The first is to "see with her own eyes the Passion" and "to suffer with him as others did who loved him." The second desire is to "have by God's gift a bodily sickness." She says she asks this so she may live more to God's glory. This may seem strange to us today, but perhaps we can understand it when we recall that Julian had experienced the plague in her youth. No doubt she watched people she loved die in pain, and desired to suffer in their place. Her longing to share Christ's passion and her wish for a bodily sickness made sense in her age, especially in light of her third prayer. In this, she desired to receive "three wounds...true contrition, loving compassion, and longing with [her] will for God." The first two prayers, sharing the Passion and the bodily sickness, are means to the third, and while she asks the first two if it were God's will, she asks the third without condition.

The revelations answered all three prayers. In them she sees Christ's passion with her own eyes, and she receives them during a bodily sickness. During the course of the visions and her long prayerful search for their meaning, she receives the three "wounds" of contrition, compassion, and longing for God in abundance.

Soon after her visions, she wrote the short text of *Showings*. The short text runs to twenty-five chapters, detailing the visions and her initial reflections on them. Fifteen to twenty years later, after receiving "inward instruction," she wrote the long text, which comprises eighty-six chapters, and then revised it. For Julian the experience of the revelation is both source and message. Consequently, she arranges her theological insights in order of the visions, and seeks to understand them not through dry intellectual reasoning alone, but with prayer and pastoral concern for her contemporaries.

Julian's theology fully integrates daily life with religious experience and theological insight. In the process, Julian dares to speculate on questions that arise, neither shying from revelations that seem to contradict church doctrine, nor dismissing church teaching. She holds both her revelations and church doctrine as authoritative, since both come from God, and seeks to reconcile them with the help of learning, reasoning, and prayer.

Her concern for orthodoxy is not motivated by fear, which would be understandable in her day, but by her pastoral concern for her even-Christians, to whom the church is mother.

Both in her experiential integration and her concern for her readers' spiritual development, Julian shows the influence of monastic theology, which made use of vivid imagery and emotional intensity. The method of this theology was rooted in *lectio divina,* the meditative and integrated reading of Scripture, which allowed the language of Scripture to permeate every aspect of life and thought. In *Wisdom's Daughter: The Theology of Julian of Norwich,* Joan Nuth writes:

> *Lectio* meant active reading, demanding full participation of body as well as mind. The words were spoken aloud so that they could be heard as well as seen, and felt by the moving of the lips. *Meditatio* meant learning by heart, i.e., with the whole body, allowing the words that were seen, heard, and felt to become fastened in the memory and understood by the intellect, so that the will might desire to put into practice the message of the words. Thus *oratio,* the petition for God, and *contemplatio,* resting in the desire for God and the fruits of this desire, were the end and goal of the *lectio* and *meditatio.*

In their critical edition of *A Book of Showings,* Colledge and Walsh note that in the long text, Julian incorporates translated phrases from the Vulgate Bible with her own sentences. It seems that her ability to think in scriptural language could well have been a result of the practice of *lectio divina.* Within this tradition, she shares with St. Francis of Assisi a deep love for Jesus, and with St. Anselm and Bernard of Clairvaux disciplined reflection arising out of this love. Her work is steeped in the biblical theology of St. Paul and St. John, and in patristic theology, especially that of Augustine. For Julian, as for these, theology was her life. As she puts it, "I saw [God] and I sought [God], I had [God] and I lacked [God], and this is and should be our ordinary undertaking in this life, as I see it" (Chapter 10). Rather than a discipline of scholars in ivory towers, theology is "our ordinary undertaking," available to all.

Julian writes to share her insights with her "even-Christians" (Chapter 8). (Although this phrase sometimes appears in translations of the *Showings* as "fellow Christians," "even-Christians" is Julian's original wording.) Accordingly, she writes her book in the vernacular, specifically the Middle English dialect of Norwich. Her language is clear and precise, and seems closer to modern English than that of her contemporary, Chaucer.

This Middle English serves her well. She makes use of words like *onyd* (united) and *homelynesse* (intimacy, familiarity), which convey her meanings more closely than their modern equivalents. She also uses inclusive language for the soul, switching pronouns from female to male and male to female (e.g., Chapter 43 and 65). Her purpose in this is clearly pastoral: she wants *all* of her even-Christians to understand that she is writing about each of their own souls. Julian's use of the expression even-Christians is another example of her linguistic accuracy. How much more inclusive and precise this is than our modern "fellow Christians"!

Julian is a master of simile, using it sparingly and creatively, avoiding clichés. Colledge and Walsh remark on her use of alliteration and rhyme. Her description of the Passion "has no rival in English literature for the vividness of detail and the intense emotional participation," writes Domenico Pezzi in his study of the theme of the Passion in Richard Rolle and Julian. For example, she says Jesus' drying skin is "of a tawny colour, like a dry board which has aged" (Chapter 17).

Her compositional skills are evident in her various revisions of her work. As she returns to write the long text, she first organizes her visions into sixteen showings, providing an outline and short description of each in Chapter 1. The short descriptions evidence her ability to consolidate much imagery and theology into spare sentences.

One-third of the long text is comprised of the material added to the fourteenth revelation. This material belongs to the third and final editing of the text, since it is not in the summary of the long text found in Chapter 1. The additions include the parable of the lord and servant and Julian's theology of God, the Mother. This material was suppressed in the short text because she could not yet fully understand it (Chapter 51). Her explanation of the parable, after twenty years of "inward instruction," displays all of Julian's gifts in their maturity.

Focus on Salvation

Julian does not set out to write a comprehensive systematic theology. Yet in the course of seeking to understand her revelations, she achieves a complete theology. In the long text especially, she considers the doctrinal implications of her insights, arranging them not by theological subject but in the order she received the visions. The result is a theology that Thomas Merton, who considered Julian to be one of the greatest English theologians, called a coherent and systematically constructed corpus of doctrine. Her achievement is particularly significant today as women theologians look for role models, and both women and men seek new ways to understand Christian doctrine.

Julian begins the exposition of her theology with her experience: "I am sure by what I feel," she writes in the long text (Chapter 40). In *Wisdom's Daughter*, Joan Nuth writes about

Julian's theology: "She trusted absolutely in her revelations as indicative of God's will for herself and the whole church."

For Julian, Christ's passion is the source, beginning, and end of all her theology. Hers is a christology of redemptive love, in which Christ on the cross says, "See how I love you." Julian begins the long text of *Showings* with these words:

> This is a revelation of love which Jesus Christ, our endless bliss, made in sixteen showings, of which the first is about his precious crowning of thorns; and in this was contained and specified the blessed Trinity, with the Incarnation and the union between God and man's soul, with many fair revelations and teachings of endless wisdom and love, in which all the revelations which follow are founded and connected.

Christ willingly undertakes the passion out of desire for union in love with us. Jesus is the suffering servant of Isaiah 53:11, sorrowing and suffering with us, out of compassion and love. Julian depicts Jesus in all his humanity, while reminding us "that he who suffered is God" (Chapter 20).

Yet suffering is not the end, for Julian says, "As I looked at the same cross, he changed to an appearance of joy. The change in his blessed appearance changed mine, and I was glad and joyful as I could possibly be" (Chapter 21). So although Julian depicts the crucifixion with all the gruesome realism of the age that endured the horror of the plague, she understands it as Christ sharing even the worst suffering of our humanity, so that we may in turn be lifted up in joyful union with God. She says, "He wishes us not to be oppressed because of the sorrows and travails which come to us, for it has always been so before the coming of miracles" (Chapter 36). Julian chooses Jesus to be her heaven, in well-being and in woe.

Julian sees Christ always in relationship with humanity. Her anthropology is profoundly optimistic, especially for her day. After the Fourth Lateran Council in 1215 set down instructions for making a proper confession, new penitential manuals appeared detailing sins and punishments. When the Black Death came it carried the fear of eternal damnation to new heights, as many died without a chance to make confessions. The plague itself was feared to be divine retribution. In this atmosphere, Julian declares, "the noblest thing which [God] ever made is [humankind]."

> [God] wants us to know that this beloved soul was preciously knitted to him in its making, by a knot so subtle and so mighty that it is united in God...all the souls which will be saved in heaven without end are knit in this knot, and united in this union, and made holy in this holiness (Chapter 53).

Julian's words in the original make the oneness of humanity and God even more clear: "united in this union" is *"onyd in this oonyng,"* "oned" in this "oneing." God "loves us and delights in us, and so [God] wishes us to love...and delight in [God]" (Chapter 68). For Julian, humans are fundamentally good. The "godly will" within us "never assented to sin and never will" (Chapter 53). Julian is even optimistic about the human body. Our physical functions are seen as good, for "[God] does not despise what [God] has made"(Chapter 6). Julian uses this surprising example:

> A man walks upright, and the food in his body is shut in as if in a well-made purse. When the time of his necessity comes, the purse is opened and then shut again, in most seemly fashion. And it is God who does this, as it

is shown when he says that he comes down to us in our humblest needs (Chapter 6).

What a deep delight Julian has in our embodiedness that she sees God even in the "seemly" workings of elimination! Unlike other writers of her day, such as Margery Kempe, Julian never even mentions chastity. Grace Jantzen credits this to Julian's "balanced and wholesome view of the physical body." Even when we die and come to God, Julian describes this in terms of the five senses: "truly seeing and wholly feeling, and hearing [God] spiritually and delectably smelling [God] and sweetly tasting [God]" (Chapter 43).

Julian saw salvation not as being redeemed from our human nature, but as being fulfilled in it. She says, "For in nature we have our life and our being, and in mercy and grace we have our increase and our fulfillment " (Chapter 56). Being made in God's image, we seek our fulfillment through "oneing" with the Love that created us. In this unity we will "know ourselves clearly" (Chapter 43).

The positive anthropology Julian develops around the revelations is most innovative and raises the most questions for Julian when she confronts the problem of sin. When Julian saw all things, she did not see sin. She realizes this means that sin has "no kind of substance, no share in being, nor can it be recognized except by the pain caused by it" (Chapter 27). She recognizes that there is pain, and sin is at work in the world. Accordingly, she wonders "why, through the great prescient wisdom of God, the beginning of sin was not prevented."

In the thirteenth revelation, Jesus says to Julian, "Sin is necessary, but all will be well, and all will be well, and every kind of thing will be well" (Chapter 27). She says that these words showed "no kind of blame to me or to anyone who will be saved." She wonders how all could be well because of the harm sin has brought to God's creatures (Chapter 29). In the answers God sends and her struggle to interpret them Julian's greatest work is born.

The Trinitarian Perspective

As noted in Chapter 31 of the long text, God begins to answer Julian's questions in this way: "I may make all things well, and I can make all things well, and I shall make all things well, and I will make all things well; and you will see yourself that every kind of thing will be well." This answer reveals a great deal about Julian's theology. God is active, expressed in verbs. Julian applies "I may" to the Father, "I can" to the Son, "I will" to the Holy Spirit, and "I shall" to the unity of the blessed Trinity.

Julian's theology is thoroughly Trinitarian, "three persons and one truth," as she puts it. But she doesn't stop with the interrelationships of the Trinity, for Julian goes on to say "when [God] says 'you will see yourself,' I understand it for the union of all...who will be saved in the blessed Trinity." God is always seen relating to humans, longing "to gather us all here into [God], to our endless joy" (Chapter 31).

Julian frequently uses triads of attributes to refer to the Trinity. The first triad cited in the showings is also the most frequent: "God almighty, all wisdom, and all love" (Chapter 1). These attributes always refer to the respective persons of the Trinity. Other triads are joy, honor, and delight (Chapter 51), and goodness, lovingness, and light.

We have seen how salvation is accomplished through our being, increase, and fulfillment, in nature, mercy, and grace (Chapter 56). The Trinity functions as Maker, Keeper, and Lover in order to accomplish this (Chapter 5). (Although Colledge and Walsh use the word "protector" in their translation, I prefer the word "keeper" found in other translations.)

Julian describes three properties which indicate God's working relationship to humanity: fatherhood, motherhood, and lordship (Chapter 58). The whole of Julian's Trinitarian theology is detailed in terms of persons, attributes, and relations. We can see this more clearly in the chart which follows (Figure 1):

FIGURE 1

Julian's Trinitarian Understanding

Person	*Verb*	*Attribute*	*Function*	*Relation*
Father	May	Might Joy Being Nature Goodness	Maker	Fatherhood
Son	Can	Wisdom Honor Increase Mercy Lovingness	Keeper	Motherhood
Holy Spirit	Will	Love Delight Fulfillment Grace Light	Lover	Lordship

The Parable of the Lord and Servant

Julian's theology reaches its highest development through her parable of the lord and servant and the understandings that follow as she ponders its meaning over many years. This parable comes as an answer to Julian's continuing questions about the paradox of sin and well-being. In the course of her exploration of its meaning, Julian's theology of motherhood is born.

In the parable, revealed in Chapter 51, Julian sees:

> two persons in bodily likeness...a lord and a servant....The servant stands before his lord, respectfully, ready to do his lord's will. The lord looks on his servant very lovingly....He sends him to a certain place to do his will. Not only does the servant go, but he dashes off and runs at great speed, loving to do his lord's will. And soon he falls into a dell and is greatly injured; and then he groans and moans and tosses about and writhes, but he cannot rise or help himself in any way. And of all this, the greatest hurt which I saw him in was lack of consolation, for he could not turn his face to look on his loving lord, who was very close to him,...but he paid heed to his...distress....
>
> I looked [for] any fault in him, or if the lord would impute to him any kind of blame; and truly none was seen....And in spirit he was as prompt and as good as he was when he stood before his lord, ready to do his will. And all this time his loving lord looks on him most tenderly...with great compassion and pity...and rejoiced over the honourable rest and nobility which...he wishes for his servant and will bring him to....And his falling and all the woe that he received from it will be turned into high, surpassing honour and endless bliss.

Julian is mystified as to what exactly the parable means, because although she understands that the lord represents God and the servant Adam, she sees characteristics in the servant that cannot refer to Adam. So she says, "For twenty years after the time of the revelation...I received an inward instruction....:You ought to take heed to all the attributes, divine and human" (Chapter 51).

As she does this, she arrives at the understanding that the servant in the parable represents Adam, one person falling who symbolizes humanity, and that God regards us with love and intends to bless us. The compassion and pity of God she relates to our humanity, but the joy and bliss were "for the falling of his dearly beloved Son." So she sees that in the example the servant is both Adam/humanity and Christ. The lord sits on barren ground, though he made the human soul to be "his own city and his dwelling place" until such time as "by his grace his beloved Son had brought back his city into its noble place of beauty by his hard labor."

She sees the servant in his threadbare tunic, yet with an inner love for the lord, equal to the lord's love for him. She says, "The wisdom of the servant saw inwardly that there was one thing to do which would pay honour to the lord"...and does it ..."for it seemed by his outer garment as if he had been a constant labourer and a hard traveller for a long time" (Chapter 51). (In their critical edition, Colledge and Walsh point out that there is a pun here between "traveller," as in journeying, and "travailer," as in the travail of childbirth, and that Julian is using the image of a woman in labor as a figure of passion, death, and resurrection.)

The labor that the servant is to do is to be a gardener, "digging and ditching and sweating and turning the soil over and over, and to dig deep down, and to water the plants at the proper time." He is to continue in travail (which is the phrase used in Julian's original text), and make sweet floods to run, and …"fine and plentious fruit to grow, which he is to bring before the lord and serve him with to his liking" (Chapter 51). Here the applications to both Adam and Jesus are clear, but Julian emphasizes the travail, repeating it three times in the passage.

In understanding the servant as the second person of the trinity, Julian sees the Son, Christ's divinity, united with his humanity, the true Adam, as "only one man." This is classic Christology: two natures in one person. Yet again Julian's words are significant for her later theology: "By the wisdom and goodness which were in the servant is understood God's Son, by the poor labourer's clothing…Adam's humanity" (Chapter 51). Here she uses the word "wisdom" a second time, having stated earlier "The wisdom of the servant saw inwardly…," and repeats this word again further on in the chapter: "…for he is the wisdom of the Father."

The repetitions of wisdom, the dwelling place, the travail, and the food the servant grows all return in Julian's motherhood simile. Nuth says, "One might expect that the lordship image for God in the parable of the lord and servant…would produce an understanding of God as patriarchal, hierarchical, and domineering," but Julian reverses that image to depict "a God content to be on equal footing with human beings.…Julian creates her picture of God by focusing upon love as God's predominant attribute."

Questions for Reflection and Discussion

1. Julian received her visions in three ways: "by bodily vision, and by words formed in [her] understanding and by spiritual vision." Have you ever experienced a sense of spiritual connection similar to any of these? What was it like? How

is Julian's phrase "I am sure by what I feel" relevant to your own spiritual life?

2. Julian's vivid description of the Passion brings the reader into "intense emotional participation" in Christ's death. What is the meaning of the Passion and crucifixion for Julian? What significance and effect does this event hold for you?

3. Julian speaks of "oneing" with God. Have you ever experienced this sense of unity with God? What does it mean for you to say "I am one with God"?

4. Julian illustrates the Trinity through a single subject and three verbs, and by using verb tenses to express the different functions of the Trinity. Do Julian's groupings of Trinitarian attributes make sense to you? What illustrations would you use?

5. Julian says she suppressed her motherhood theology in the short text because she did not yet understand it. Do you think she might have had additional reasons? Have you ever suppressed insights or innovations you have had? Why? If you eventually shared them, what changed to allow you to do this?

CHAPTER FIVE

Julian's Theology of Motherhood

Immediately following her exposition of the lord and servant parable, Julian says, "And so I saw that God rejoices that he is our Father, and God rejoices that he is our Mother" (Chapter 52). The reference to Mother strikes us as abrupt, especially since it is an unequivocal title for God, not a simile.

Julian starts to unfold her Motherhood theology in Chapter 54. She begins, as we might expect, with its place in the Trinity: "And the deep wisdom of the Trinity is our Mother, in whom we are enclosed." She moves on to show how "our savior is our true Mother, in whom we are endlessly born and out of whom we shall never come" (Chapter 57). "In our Mother Christ we profit and increase, and in mercy he reforms and restores us and by the power of his Passion, his death, and his

Resurrection he unites us to our substance" (Chapter 58). Julian explains that "Jesus is our true Mother in nature by our first creation, and he is our true Mother in grace by his taking our created nature" (Chapter 59).

Julian connects Jesus' suffering on the cross with a mother's birth pains (Chapter 60):

> Our true Mother Jesus, he alone bears us for joy and for endless life, blessed may he be. So he carries us within him in love and travail, until the full time when he wanted to suffer the sharpest thorns and cruel pains that ever were or will be, and at the last he died. And when he had finished, and had borne us so for bliss, still all this could not satisfy his wonderful love.

Like a nursing mother, Jesus feeds "us with himself...with the blessed sacrament" (Chapter 60). Jesus mothers us not only in birth but throughout our lives, giving us a "mother's love in well-being and in woe" (Chapter 61). "And always as the child grows in stature, she acts differently, but she does not change her love" (Chapter 60).

Julian then speaks of "our mother Holy Church, who is Christ Jesus," asking us to go "to Holy Church, into our Mother's breast, that is to say into our own soul, where our Lord dwells" (Chapter 62). Julian summarizes her motherhood teaching in Chapter 63 of the long text.

Where did all this mother imagery come from? Julian did not invent this theme. She stands in line with a long tradition of mother imagery found in the scriptures of both Judaism and Christianity. From earliest biblical times, through patristic writers in the first century to Julian's medieval contemporaries, the motherhood simile has served to express divine love.

God is likened to a mother in many places in Hebrew Scripture. In the Pentateuch, God is compared to a mother eagle teaching her young to fly (Exodus 19:4, Deuteronomy 32:11). Mother imagery occurs in Psalm 131:2 (a mother comforting her child); Isaiah 42:14 (a woman in labor); Isaiah 46:3-4 (God will bear, carry, and save, a direct reference, not a simile); Isaiah 49:15 (a nursing mother showing compassion for her child); and Isaiah 66:13 (a mother comforting her child). We can see themes emerging in these references: God is like a woman in labor, bearing children; God is like a nursing mother; God comforts the people as a mother comforts her child.

Wisdom is personified as a woman throughout the Wisdom writings of Hebrew Scriptures. Joan Nuth writes in *Wisdom's Daughter:*

> There Wisdom is a female figure who existed before the beginning of the world (Proverbs 8:22-31) and who is associated with the act of creation: "The Lord by Wisdom founded the earth" (Proverbs 3:19). She is also responsible for the work of recreation "while remaining in herself, she renews all things" (Wisdom 7:27), and the work of salvation: "the paths of those on earth were set right, and [they] were saved by Wisdom" (Wisdom 9:18). She is involved in the work of sanctification "in every generation she passes into holy souls and makes them friends of God and prophets" (Wisdom 7:27).

In the lament over Jerusalem (Matthew 23:37-39 and Luke 13:34-35), Jesus likens himself to a mother hen, drawing upon a long tradition of mother bird imagery. (See Deuteronomy 32:11, Exodus 19:4, Ruth 2:12, Psalms 17:8, 36:7, 91:1-4, and Isaiah 31:5.) These images often occur along with the name

Shaddai (Almighty) or *El Shaddai* (God almighty) containing the Hebrew root *shad* (breast). In Luke 11:49, Wisdom admonishes the people, and the Matthean parallel passage is just before the lament, linking Wisdom with the imagery of Jesus as mother hen. In fact, it appears that in the lament Jesus is speaking *as* Wisdom.

Jesus also speaks of wisdom in Luke 7:35. The woman with a lost coin, found in Luke 15:3–10, while not a mother image, is a feminine image parallel to the shepherd and the father in the framing parables. In John 3:4–6, the Holy Spirit gives birth, and in John 5:21 the Creator and the Son give life. Jesus calls those who thirst to come to him and drink, invoking nursing imagery. Jesus refers to the disciples as "little children" in John 13:33, and in John 16:21–22 they are likened to a woman in labor.

Birthgiving imagery appears in 1 John 3:9, and nursing imagery in 1 Corinthians 3:1–2, in which Paul feeds milk to infants in Christ, and in Hebrews 5:12: "You need milk." Birth and nursing imagery are combined in 1 Peter 1:23–2:3. Paul refers to Jesus Christ as Wisdom in 1 Corinthians 1:24, "Christ the power of God and the wisdom of God" and 1 Corinthians 1:30, "Christ Jesus, who became for us wisdom from God."

Mother imagery continues in patristic writings. In her book *Jesus as Mother,* Caroline Walker Bynum says, "The writings of Clement, Origen, Irenaeus, John Chrysostom, Ambrose, and Augustine all describe Christ as mother." Clement writes, "And God Himself is love; and out of love to us became feminine." He depicts Christ in mother bird imagery, and also as a nursing mother. Origen refers to Paul's identification of Christ as Wisdom. St. John Chrysostom uses mother bird imagery and womb imagery, and develops the nursing mother image, referring to the eucharist as "the nipple of the spiritual cup."

Ambrose depicts the two Testaments as the breasts of the Son, nourishing us on spiritual milk, and speaks of Christ as "the virgin who carried us in her womb, gave birth to us, and fed us with her own milk." St. Augustine equates Christ with Wisdom and combines this with the mother hen image, urging us to "fly to the wings of Mother Wisdom." He also cites Wisdom 10:1-2, in which "She *(Sapientia)* preserved Adam, brought him out of his sin and gave him lordship of all things." Augustine applies wisdom to the nursing mother imagery as well, speaking of Christ converting his wisdom into milk for our benefit, and depicts himself as suckled on Christ's milk.

Medieval scholastic writers emphasized Christ as Wisdom, using maternal imagery. Bynum cites Peter Lombard, Abelard, Albert the Great, Thomas Aquinas, and Bonaventure in this regard. Bonaventure continues the suckling imagery, and Albert the Great says, "The Wisdom of God is the first mother in whose womb we have been formed." Thomas Aquinas includes the motherhood analogy in his *Catena Aurea,* citing Augustine and John Chrysostom. The *Ancrene Riwle* and Richard Rolle also use mother imagery.

Maternal imagery flourished in the writings of medieval monastic authors. Anselm of Canterbury, Bernard of Clairvaux, Aelred of Rievaulx, Guerric of Igny, Isaac of Stella, Adam of Perseigne, Helinand of Froidmont, and William of St. Thierry carry on this tradition in the twelfth century. Anselm says, "And you, my soul...run under the wing of Jesus your mother and lament your griefs under his feathers." Bernard exhorts young monks to "suck...the breasts of the crucified....He will be your mother, and you will be his son." Guerric says Christ is "a mother, too, in the mildness of his affection, and a nurse," and likens the Holy Spirit to milk from Christ's breasts. William of St. Thierry applies mother imagery to Christ, and nursing imagery to the work of grace.

Bynum attributes the use of maternal imagery among twelfth-century male monastic writers to "the rise of affective spirituality and the feminization of religious language." These trends grew out of a need to emphasize the approachability of God and affirm the goodness of creation. They reflect an increasing eucharistic piety and a need among male monastic communities to supplement authority with nurturing love. Bynum says, "Every Cistercian author in whose writings maternal imagery plays a prominent role was himself an abbot."

Twelfth- through fourteenth-century women writers also used maternal imagery. These women were not, for the most part, abbesses although some did advise others. Many were visionaries to whom God spoke directly. Mechtild of Hackborn, Bridget of Sweden, and Catherine of Siena elaborate on the theme of Isaiah 66:13 and depict Christ as a mother playfully hiding from her child. Margaret d'Oyngt, who was a prioress, depicts Christ's birthpangs, and Margery Kempe has an anchorite tell her, "Dowtyr, ye sowkyn euyn on Crystys brest" (Daughter, you suckle even on Christ's breast).

In *Piers the Ploughman,* William Langland invites us to "feed in safety at [Christ's] breast," and Julian's contemporary, the Monk of Farne says, "Do not wean me, good Jesus, from the breasts of thy consolation" (an allusion to Isaiah 66:11). Margaret d'Oyngt summarizes the affective character of devotion to Jesus as mother in the twelfth through fourteenth centuries: Christ says, "My luffe schalle be thy modere...ande she schalle helpe the ande comforth the als a luffynge modere helpys ande conforthtys here douwter in alle tyme of nede" (My love shall be thy mother...and she shall help thee and comfort thee as a loving mother helps and comforts her daughter in all time of need).

These references, by no means exhaustive, show the scope of the precedent for Julian's motherhood similitude. In "*God is Our Mother*": *Julian of Norwich and the Medieval Image of Christian Feminine Divinity,* Jennifer P. Heimmel says,

> Such an extensive background for this tradition…ranging through…biblical, patristic, and mystical literature, points to its own conclusion. Julian's beliefs…concerning a feminine and maternal God must be seriously considered as part of a lengthy and orthodox Christian tradition.

Julian develops all of these themes—images of Christ as a woman in labor, related to Christ's passion; nursing-mother imagery related to the Eucharist; imagery of Christ as a comforting, nurturing mother; and wisdom-imagery—in her motherhood simile. She uses these images extensively, systematizing them, relating them to one another, summarizing the entire motherhood tradition, and making Christ as mother the summary image of her soteriology (theology of salvation).

Themes of the Motherhood Theology

In Chapter 52, Julian introduces her motherhood theology in this way:

> And so I saw that God rejoices that he is our Father and God rejoices that he is our Mother, and God rejoices that he is our true spouse, and that our soul is his beloved wife. And Christ rejoices that he is our brother, and Jesus rejoices that he is our saviour.

For Julian, all of these images are related and pertain to her motherhood theology. Creation itself, our re-creation in Christ, the mutual indwelling of God and humankind, Christ's incarnation, and salvation through Jesus Christ are all integral elements of Julian's theology of motherhood.

She begins her exposition of this theology with a figure of wisdom: "And the deep wisdom of the Trinity is our Mother, in whom we are enclosed" (Chapter 54). How does she arrive at the figure of wisdom? Just after introducing the motherhood theme, Julian says, "We have in us a marvellous mixture of both well-being and woe. We have in us our risen Lord Jesus Christ, and we have in us the wretchedness and the harm of Adam's falling" (Chapter 52). This obviously refers to Julian's parable of the lord and servant, in which the servant represents both Christ and Adam.

If we look back at the passages about the servant in Chapter 51 (also see p. 39), we find him identified with wisdom: "The wisdom of the servant saw inwardly"; "By the wisdom and goodness which were in the servant is understood God's Son"; and "Very truly the Son knew when was the Father's will...for he is the wisdom of the Father." Julian's identification of wisdom as the savior of Adam has a scriptural basis. Wisdom 10:1 says, "Wisdom protected the first-formed father of the world, when he alone had been created; she delivered him from his transgression."

Julian is deeply familiar with the Book of Wisdom, and we find allusions to it throughout the above passages: Wisdom 8:17, "When I considered these things inwardly"; Wisdom 7:26, "For she is an image of [God's] goodness"; Wisdom 9:9, "With you is wisdom, she who knows your works." Wisdom 9:18 says, "And thus the paths of those on earth were set right, and people were taught what pleases you, and were saved by wisdom." So Julian, very naturally, identifies Christ the savior with wisdom, with precedent in St. Paul (1 Corinthians 1:24; 30), and patristic and medieval writers, as we have seen.

Wisdom is called Mother in Wisdom 7:12, and in Sirach 24:18 she says, "I am the mother of beautiful love, of fear, of knowledge, and of holy hope" (this verse appears as a footnote to the text in many contemporary versions of Scripture). Colledge and Walsh cite verse 25 of Sirach 24 (found in the Vulgate, but not in the New Revised Standard Version): "In me is all grace of the way and of the truth...all hope of life," words which Christ applies to himself in John 14:6. Julian follows these connections when she identifies wisdom as Mother and Christ.

Julian mentions wisdom in Chapter 53 as well: "wise in mind of the wisdom of the Son." This chapter deals with the mutual indwelling of God and humankind: the Trinity is "the mediator," "the foundation...out of whom we have all come, in whom we are all enclosed, into whom we shall all go." She ends the chapter with the image of our soul being knit to God with a knot so subtle and so mighty that it is "onyd" (united) to God. The knitting imagery echoes Psalm 139:13: "You knit me together in my mother's womb."

Enclosure is not only a womb image, but for Julian would also connote anchoritic enclosure. In the lord and servant parable, the servant is "a constant labourer and a hard traveller for a long time" (Chapter 51). Julian connects this womb imagery with Adam and Christ, saying, "God's son fell with Adam, into the valley of the womb of the maiden who was the fairest daughter of Adam" (Chapter 51). This is the imagery she expands in Chapter 53 with the mutual enclosure language, and returns to it as she unfolds the wisdom theology of Chapter 54.

When Julian unites wisdom, motherhood, and the womb in Chapter 54, she echoes Albert the Great (see p. 45). Julian expands this into our enclosure within the Trinity and the Trinity's enclosure in us. In this "oneing," Julian says, "in that same instant and place in which our soul is made sensual...exists the city of God, ordained for him from without beginning" (Chapter 55). "That honourable city in which our Lord Jesus sits is our sensuality, in which he is enclosed, and our natural substance is enclosed in Jesus, with the blessed soul of Christ sitting in rest in the divinity" (Chapter 56). Julian brings wisdom into this passage by scriptural allusion: she says "our good Lord himself leads us into this high depth." According to Colledge and Walsh, this remarkable phrase, "high depth," is a quote from Ecclesiastes 7:24–25, in which Koheleth (the Preacher) says, "I have tried all things in wisdom....It is a high deepness."

Julian continues the womb imagery and wisdom allusions in Chapter 56: "These are our foundations, in which we have our being, our increase, and our fulfillment. For in nature we have our life and our being, and in mercy and grace we have our increase and our fulfillment." Proverbs 3:19 says, "The Lord by wisdom founded the earth," so Julian's use of the word "foundations" is an allusion to wisdom, which appears in the last sentence of this chapter. "In which we have our being" quotes Acts 17:28: "For in [God] we live and move and have our being," another womb image.

Julian extends this scriptural image in Chapter 57: "Our saviour is our true Mother, in whom we are endlessly born and out of whom we shall never come," placing it alongside a reference to Mary which connects the Incarnation and our life in Christ. Julian relates this connection to her first revelation, which speaks of enclosure, and her sixteenth, in which Christ sits in our soul (the city of God, Chapter 57). The *perichoresis* (interweaving) of the Trinity, the meaning of the Incarnation, and the reign of Christ within us are all summarized in the deeply scriptural imagery of our Mother's womb.

The descriptive triad "being, increase and fulfillment" return in Chapter 58, in which Julian details her Trinitarian theology. Having identified God almighty as our loving Father, God all Wisdom as our loving Mother, and the Holy Spirit with love and goodness, Julian says, "In the first we have our being, and in the second we have our increasing, and in the third we have our fulfillment. The first is nature, the second is mercy, and the third is grace" (Chapter 58).

Julian says, "In the second person, in knowledge and wisdom we have our perfection (kepyng), as regards our sensuality, our restoration, and our salvation, for he is our Mother, brother, and saviour" (Chapter 58). In this passage are allusions to Wisdom 7:27: "she renews all things," and Wisdom 9:18: "saved by wisdom," as well as to a phrase from Mechtild of Hackborn in which Christ says, "I am...a modere in redempcion" (I am...a mother in redemption). Julian describes the working of our Mother as including Christ's Passion: "In our mother Christ we profit and increase, and in mercy he reforms and restores us, and by the power of his Passion, his death, and his Resurrection he unites (onyd) us to our substance" (Chapter 58).

Having thus laid the foundation, Julian builds her motherhood theology in Chapter 59: "So Jesus Christ, who opposes good to evil, is our true Mother. We have our being from him, where the foundation of motherhood begins, with all the sweet protection of love which endlessly follows." Julian says, "as truly as God is our Father, so truly is God our Mother." In this chapter and the next three, Julian unfolds her mother imagery to its highest development:

Jesus is our true Mother in nature by our first creation, and he is our true Mother in grace by his taking our created nature. All the lovely works and all the sweet loving offices of beloved motherhood are appropriated to the second person.

Continuing on in Chapter 59, Julian then proposes a framework for systematizing her motherhood theology: "I understand three ways of contemplating motherhood in God. The first is the foundation of our nature's creation; the second is...taking of our nature, where the motherhood of grace begins; the third is the motherhood at work." She ties these categories together with: "by the same grace, everything is penetrated (forth spredyng), in length and in breadth, in height and in depth without end; and it is all one love." We will return to this framework after surveying Julian's motherhood imagery.

In Chapter 60, Julian says that we were "created by the motherhood of love." "Our great God, the supreme (soueryn) wisdom of all things, arrayed...himself to do the service and office of motherhood in everything." This is like Clement's statement about God becoming feminine (see p. 44). "The mother's service is nearest, readiest, and surest," Julian says, emphasizing the quality of approachability so important to medieval spirituality.

Julian then makes the connection between Christ's Passion and a mother's birth pains. She moves from that directly into nursing imagery:

The mother can give her child suck of her milk, but our precious Mother Jesus can feed us with himself, and does, most courteously and most tenderly with the blessed sacrament, which is the precious food of true life (Chapter 60).

Julian's nursing imagery stands in line with the long tradition going back to Isaiah's simile in 49:15, through patristic writers like Ambrose, to medievals like Bonaventure and Bernard. She brings this nursing imagery together with the "oneing" aspect of the womb imagery in a passage (Chapter 60) that sounds strange to our modern ears, less used to mystical imagery than Julian's contemporaries:

> The mother can lay her child tenderly to her breast, but our tender Mother Jesus can lead us easily into his blessed breast through his sweet open side, and show us there a part of the godhead and of the joys of heaven, with inner certainty of endless bliss.

Julian praises "this fair lovely word 'mother'," and says "To the property of motherhood belong nature, love, wisdom and knowledge, and this is God" (Chapter 60). Having introduced God's Motherhood through wisdom, and having led us through womb imagery and birthing imagery to nursing imagery, Julian moves on to describe the motherhood at work throughout our lives, comforting and nurturing us:

> The kind loving mother who knows and sees the need of her child guards it very tenderly, as the nature and condition of motherhood will have. And always as the child grows in age and stature, she acts differently, but she does not change her love.

This sentiment echoes a long tradition, from Isaiah 66:13 through medievals like Margaret d'Oyngt.

Julian, with her deeply scriptural thinking, links our love for God as mother to the commandment to honor thy father and mother (Exodus 20:12), saying that we fulfill this commandment in truly loving God! She speaks of God's unconditional love in Chapter 61: "that love which cannot and will not be broken because of offenses," and alludes to John 3:16: "And though our earthly mother may suffer her child to perish, our heavenly Mother Jesus may never suffer us who are his children to perish, for he is almighty, all wisdom, and all love." Julian speaks of our mother letting us experience falling, for our own benefit, and says "Our courteous Mother does not wish us to flee away...but...to behave like a child. For when it is distressed and frightened, it runs quickly to its mother," echoing Augustine and Anselm. We are to trust in our "mother's love in well-being and in woe," which we find in "the faith of Holy Church."

As she speaks of Holy Church, Julian returns to nursing imagery: it is good for us to will "to be fastened and united (onyd) to our mother Holy Church, who is Christ Jesus," bringing in the sacrament with a reference to Christ's blood and water (Chapter 61). In Chapter 62 she connects this nursing imagery with her mutual indwelling city of God image: we need to "go to Holy Church, into our Mother's breast, that is to say into our own soul, where our Lord dwells."

Chapter 63 summarizes Julian's motherhood theology, revisiting motherhood themes: wisdom, "In our true Mother Jesus our life is founded in his own prescient wisdom from without beginning"; birthing, "on the cross he bore us to endless life"; nursing, "he feeds us"; and comforting, "and fosters us, just as the great supreme lovingness (souereyne kyndnesse) of motherhood wishes." "Naturally the child loves the mother and either of them the other," Julian says. She repeats the revelation which began her long contemplation leading to the parable of the lord and servant and the motherhood teaching: "All will be well, and you will see it yourself, that every kind of thing will be well," echoing Wisdom 8:1: "She orders all things well." Julian ends these teachings with "And the bliss of our motherhood in Christ be to begin anew in the joys of our Father, God, which new beginning will last, newly beginning without end."

Julian has come full circle, and brought us through the motherhood simile to the bliss of our continual birthing in heaven. She reiterates this at the very end of her book: "So I was taught that love is our Lord's meaning....In this love we have our beginning, and all this shall we see in God without end" (Chapter 86).

Julian's systematic presentation of motherhood imagery is illustrated on the following page (Figure 2). Her categories— foundation, taking our nature/motherhood of grace, and the motherhood at work—are combined with the thematic categories we have explored in her predecessors: birthing, nursing, and comforting/nurturing. To this group is added wisdom, which introduces Julian's motherhood theme and links it to the second person of the Trinity, and fulfillment, to which all of this imagery leads: salvation, "the bliss of our motherhood in Christ" (Chapter 63).

Julian's purpose in her theological endeavor is to love Christ better. From her first prayers, through her revelations which answered them, and many years of scriptural and theological study, Julian desires "to know...what was our Lord's meaning." The result is a systematic theology that synthesizes Julian's personal experience of revelation and insights from the entire Christian tradition.

Her theology is warm and human, answering the needs of her contemporaries for an approachable theology and affirmation of the goodness of creation. Especially in her treatment of the motherhood simile, she advances theological thought considerably. Julian's achievement in the fourteenth century is remarkable. In the next chapter, we will look at her relevance to theology today.

Figure 2: **Julian's Theology of Motherhood**

Foundation *Chapter 59*	Taking our nature/Mother- hood of Grace *Chapter 59*	The Motherhood at work *Chapter 59*

Wisdom	**Birthing**	**Nursing**	**Comforting/ Nurturing**
Second person of the Trinity *Chapter 54*	We are founded and rooted *Chapter 56*	Jesus feeds us with himself: the blessed Sacrament of	In our mother, we profit and increase; he reforms us &
Loving Mother *Chapter 58*	We are enclosed in our mother Christ,	Holy Church *Chapter 60*	restores us *Chapter 58*
In second per- son, knowledge and wisdom, is our perfection, restoration, salvation *Chapter 58*	and mother Christ in us *Chapter 53, 54* We are Christ's children *Chapter 54*	Holy Church is our Mother's breast: our soul, where our Lord dwells *Chapter 62*	As the child grows, the mother acts dif- ferently, but she does not change her love *Chapter 60*
	Mother's womb *Chapter 60*	Flood of mercy: Christ's blood and water *Chapter 61, 63*	Mother letting child fall, child runs to mother *Chapter 61*
	In which we have our being *Chapter 58, 59*	Mother Jesus leads us into his blessed breast *Chapter 60*	Unconditional love *Chapter 61*
	City of God, our soul, where our Lord dwells *Chapter 58, 57*	Mother in grace by taking our nature *Chapter 59*	Fosters us, brings us up *Chapter 63*
	Mother of life and of all things *Chapter 60*		

= Salvation

All will be well	Bliss of the motherhood in Christ Newly beginning without end *Chapter 63*	Joys of God

In this Love we have our beginning, and all this shall we see in God without end (Ch. 86).

Questions for Reflection and Discussion

1. How does Julian's imagery of the Savior as "our true Mother in whom we are endlessly born and out of whom we shall never come" differ from your previous understanding of Christ as Savior? What do you think Julian means by "our motherhood in Christ?" How would Christianity be different if this was a predominant teaching?

2. Why did early church fathers like Augustine use female imagery for Christ? Does God seem more approachable to you in female terms? Why or why not?

3. How does the sacrament of eucharist relate to images of a nursing mother? Does this change your perception about the sacrament when you hear it described this way?

4. Why do you think wisdom is personified as a woman? How does it feel to think of Jesus in female wisdom imagery? Does this imagery ring true with what you know of Jesus, or is it new and different?

5. Julian locates the dwelling place of God in our sensuality. Does this resonate with your understanding of sensuality? Your image of God? How would society be different if we saw our sensuality in this way?

CHAPTER SIX

Julian's Theology for Today

The fourteenth century was a time of great change. As Anna Maria Reynolds writes in *Julian: Woman of Our Day,* it was "an unstable and violent world, more inclined to pessimism than optimism." Society was becoming increasingly urban, and feudal institutions were collapsing.

We, too, live in an unstable, violent world. The twentieth century has experienced the greatest rate of change in history. Social institutions are collapsing or radically changing. Our economic situation is in flux as we move from a technological reliance on abundant natural resources to a world in which resources are increasingly scarce, and ecological disaster threatens. The rapid rate of change and the breakup of social institutions create a need for grounding and centering.

Julian lived in times much like our own, and her theology speaks clearly to our needs today. As in Julian's day, the need for centering leads some to the contemplative life. Amid the rapid pace of the twentieth century, the monastic tradition provides refuge, as it did in Julian's times. One of those who followed this path yet remained in touch with his contemporaries was Thomas Merton. Merton's books, like Julian's, are personal meditations offered to all. Their popularity attests to the hunger in our times for spiritual renewal.

Significantly, in his quest for spirituality, Merton turns to Julian. In the book *Conjectures of a Guilty Bystander,* he writes, "I pray much to have a wise heart, and perhaps the rediscovery of Lady Julian of Norwich will help me." Merton was impressed by Julian's realism, citing her admission that there is no intellectual solution to the problem of evil even as she trusts that all will be well. It is Julian's ability to relate her spiritual insights to the real lives of people that led Merton to seek her centering wisdom.

In the face of change, Julian gives us a theology that is grounded in the entire Christian tradition, yet centered in her experience as a woman. "The deep wisdom of the Trinity is our Mother, in whom we are enclosed" (Chapter 54). Living in the womb of the Mother, what can harm us? It is a deeply reassuring image. In the midst of her violent age, Julian speaks words of wisdom: "All will be well, and all will be well, and every kind of thing will be well " (Chapter 27). Too many people today have exactly the opposite impression. Seeking death becomes seductive, since too often we feel all is doomed. Julian's words of well-being, uttered in the midst of her own century's pessimism, speak to our hearts today.

In an age when we are at the brink of environmental destruction, Julian gives us the vision of the world as small as a hazelnut, with her interpretation that God is present in all things, and all is done by God's prescient wisdom (Chapters

5 and 11). In the face of the alienation of her day and of ours, Julian sees the "oneing" between the divine and all creation, including ourselves (Chapter 53). As we face the persecutions, plagues, wars, and destruction which have marked this century, we have great need for a comforting, nurturing theology. Julian's description of the motherhood at work, nurturing us, raising us up, giving us unconditional love, meets these needs. In the grace of this love, all is permeated, "in length and in breadth, in height and in depth without end, and it is all one love" (Chapter 59).

In the fourteenth century there was need of spiritual renewal and unity in a divided church. During Julian's lifetime there was a period when two popes ruled over the church, and another in which three popes claimed rights to the chair of Peter.

The institutional Christian church of the twentieth century has struggled to cope with social change. It has fragmented into many denominations, and tension within these strain their cohesion. Many people deny the spiritual realm entirely, while some religionists deny the physical realm. Unity seems less attainable than ever, even as our longing for it grows. We search for a theology that is truly universal, one that resolves the tensions between the spiritual and physical realms. There is a longing for mysticism, for introversion in our extroverted culture. We seek spirituality with personal relevance for our lives.

Through all this, Julian leads us to Holy Church in our Mother's breast, in our own soul (Chapter 62). In doing so, she leads us to the wellspring of our own mystical experience as a source for spiritual renewal. Thomas Merton, who also reflects deeply upon his personal experience, praises Julian's "synthesis of mystical experience and theological reflection" in his book *Mystics and Zen Masters*.

Julian's spirituality and theology begin with her own experience, which she trusts completely: "I am sure by what I feel," she says (Chapter 40). Her theology integrates experience and scholarship, achieving a synthesis that brings new wisdom. In her method as in her conclusions, Julian demonstrates her relevance to our needs today, bringing forth change from within a process that is her life.

A Theology in Context

Exactly what is Julian's method? How does she move from her mystical experience to a systematic theology addressing the needs of her day?

Julian begins with her vision. We have seen earlier how the anchorite life-style encouraged mystical experiences and reflection. Julian's vision arises in the midst of an illness, when, at the point of death, she fixes her gaze upon the crucifix, identifying with Jesus in his last hours. Such visions are not uncommon in individuals who are at the point of death, but Julian's is unusual in its length and detail, and in her precise memory of each part. Her training in *lectio divina* would have contributed to her ability to remember the words and details of her vision. Confident that her vision is a message from God, she writes the short text of the *Showings* soon after she recovers from her illness, and begins to reflect upon the visions, seeking to understand them not for herself alone, but with pastoral concern for her even-Christians.

As she contemplates the meaning of her vision, Julian searches Scripture for guidance. The extent of the scriptural borrowings in her writing attest to the fruits of this labor. While she puts her own experience first, Julian's second source is her tradition, including the written scriptural record, writings of those who preceded her in the tradition, and her experience of the living tradition in active worship. Julian's scholarship serves to root and ground her mystical direct experience of the divine in the larger tradition which shapes the worldview of her contemporaries.

Having recorded her visions and researched their background in tradition, Julian's next step is to integrate the theology that emerges into the daily life and experiences of her readers. She is cautious in this process, as her twenty-year period of inward instruction about the parable of the lord and servant attests. Until she fully understands a concept to the point that she is able to express it clearly to others, she refrains from communication. She ponders in her heart the discrepancy between the blame for sin which the teachings of the church assign to humankind, and the blamelessness in which God holds us in her vision (Chapter 50), until she arrives at the solution: "we are brought back by the motherhood of mercy and grace into our natural place, in which we were created by the motherhood of love, a mother's love which never leaves us " (Chapter 60).

In the motherhood simile, Julian finds an image which speaks to the experience of all, since all have their being through the gift of a mother. It is the need to communicate her understanding of the vision to her contemporaries that leads Julian to this image, which was not part of her original vision. It is this that gives Julian's work such power to transcend the limits of time and place. She is not content to keep her understanding to herself, or even within the teachings of her tradition, but ventures beyond her own needs to reach for a universal image that can speak to all. For Julian, and I believe for us, the motherhood simile is that universal image.

In contemporary Christianity, there are others who have similarly instructed the faithful through their own experiences and insights. One such visionary is Lee Carlton, a pastor in the Metropolitan Community Church. This ecumenical community has a particular ministry to gays and lesbians, who are often treated as outcasts of society much as were those afflicted by the Black Death in the fourteenth century. Perhaps more than most, communities such as this have a great need of a comforting, nurturing, positive theology.

Like Julian, Carlton received his vision when he was thirty years old, on February 4, 1977. The vision is told in immediate, personal language, with vivid details, in much the same fashion as Julian's. Carlton says:

I saw the three faces of God, moving continually one over the other, translucent. All were both masculine and feminine. A feminine voice said, "My child, do you know how many there be in the world who have need of thee? Come here and put your mouth on my breast gently." Then I floated, and became like a little child, at my mother's breast....A substance flowed into my body, and my ears were unstopped, and I could hear in a dimension that wasn't there before....I saw the universe, like a dark starry night, and images came....There was light in arcs going out all over the planet.

Like Julian, Carlton questions whether the vision is genuine, and looks to Scripture for understanding of the revelation. He finds Scripture describing the Word of God as milk (1 Peter 2:2), as well as Paul's words in Galatians 3:28: "In Christ there is neither male nor female."

Carlton's theology of his vision develops within the gay and lesbian community, a group torn by plague and persecution. Just as the bubonic plague did in the fourteenth century, the modern-day plague of AIDS has led to persecution of the groups popularly identified with the disease. Theologies of divine retribution which blame people with AIDS for their disease as punishment for their sins recall the persecutions of Jews and the witch-hunts prevalent during the Black Death.

Amid the pessimism of our own age, Carlton, like Julian, arrives at an overwhelmingly positive theology in which all creation is seen as good and loved by God, and our sexuality as a gift from God. Far from seeing humanity as evil, Julian speaks of the nobility of humankind. She locates the city of God not only in humanity, but specifically in our sensuality. How different this is than the negative theologies of Julian's day and our own! Rather than blaming our sensuality for our illness and disillusion, Julian exalts our sensuality as God's dwelling place, and expresses this in the womb imagery of mutual divine/human enclosure.

As Julian trusts that "all will be well" meanwhile aware that this is not yet so, Lee Carlton, a man who himself is living with AIDS, says "I am healed" though this is not yet fully accomplished. Both Julian and Carlton claim positive results even when in the midst of pain. Julian says God "wishes us not to be oppressed because of the sorrows and travails which come to us, for it has always been so before the coming of miracles" (Chapter 36).

As Julian's motherhood theology serves as the highest expression of God's love, so the divine feminine in Lee Carlton's vision expresses God's love to a group living as outcasts today. As in Julian's theology, the mother imagery in Carlton's vision serves to emphasize the nearness of God's love, reaching us in our embodiment as God's children.

Julian and Feminist Spirituality
Julian's motherhood theology is especially powerful for contemporary women. In our day, as in Julian's, many women feel increasingly alienated from church hierarchy and institutions. The core symbols of Christianity, as well, have become inadequate for many women. Joan Nuth says, "feminist religious scholars have concluded that the Christian theological tradition has been produced from an overwhelmingly androcentric bias, and Christian women in every age have had to live with symbols created and perpetuated by men."

A great many women have voiced this concern in the last twenty years. Sally Gearhart, speaking in the early days of the modern women's movement, was more emphatic: "Traditional Christian concepts are the constructs of male thinking and depend for their perpetuation upon a myth of male superiority." "Can a woman be saved by a male Savior?" asks Jann Aldredge-Clanton in her recent book *In Search of the Christ-Sophia*. Unfortunately, for many women an exclusively male savior reinforces the stereotype of weakness and helplessness that we grew up with: "Help, save me!" cries the stereotypical woman in distress, and a stereotypical male figure enters the scene, crying "Here I come to save the day!"

In her book *Women's Spirituality: Resources for Christian Development*, Joann Wolski Conn says, "If a woman's God-image works to reinforce a lack of self-esteem and restrict hope, she must drop that God-image." Not only does exclusively male Christ-imagery disillusion women, it also limits "Christ's living within and ministering through women," says Aldredge-Clanton. These limits are both external, as in churches which refuse women the priesthood because they don't resemble the image of Christ, and internal, in which women don't see themselves in Christ.

Women need to see themselves in the image of the divine and to approach theology from their own experience. Because Christianity's God-imagery has been propagated as overwhelmingly male, many women have sought the feminine divine elsewhere. Others have become involved in reconstructing Christianity, exploring fluidity of gender within Christianity's core symbols. Both of these approaches begin with women considering their own experience.

"I am on a journey: back into time, forward into the future, down into my center." With these words, Jean Mountaingrove, one of the founders of *WomanSpirit* magazine, sums up (in language worthy of Julian) both her own spiritual quest and the theological focus of many women today. *WomanSpirit* magazine, collectively published from 1974-1984 in Wolf Creek, Oregon, reflects the women's spirituality movement in the heady days following its inception. All kinds of women wrote here, for one another, of their spiritual journeys. In the first issue they expressed their quest:

> This is a crucial time for women. We have begun to understand and work through much of our oppression. We have made radical changes in our lives—and we are becoming aware of the immensity of these changes....We know that patriarchy cannot withstand our changes; something is going to happen. We are feeling stirrings inside us that tell us that what we are making is nothing less than a new culture.

This call to a new spirituality reached me over twenty years ago, in my youth. Through this inaugural issue of *WomanSpirit*, I read for the first time other women's words that expressed experiences like mine. For me, as for many of us, the divine spoke in a female voice, giving me hope and strength. With my experience affirmed by other women, I sought and found the divine Mother in Goddess spirituality, arising from the oldest traditions of humankind. This spirituality—centering, positive, and affirming—was born of the experience of women.

Like Margery Kempe seeking out Julian, I sought confirmation and encouragement in the wisdom of older women who were teachers to me. As the motherhood image did for Julian, the image of the Goddess brought forth new possibilities as women like myself and my teachers began to see the divinity within ourselves, and experience ourselves as actively participating in creation. Early in the women's movement, we began to move in the same direction Julian did: toward the Mother.

Searching for the divine feminine within Christianity, Scripture scholar Elisabeth Schüssler Fiorenza finds the ancient religion of the Goddess integrated with the beginnings of the Wisdom tradition. In an article titled "The Sophia-God of Jesus and the Discipleship of Women," she writes:

> It is inspired by a positive attempt of speak in the language of its own culture and to integrate elements of its Goddess [tradition], especially of Isis worship, into Jewish monotheism...that is, it uses elements of Goddess-language in order to speak of the gracious goodness of Israel's God in the language of the Goddess.

Here the common roots of Goddess-spirituality and feminist Judaism and Christianity can be seen. The experience of the divine Mother transcends all theological divisions, and arises in the heart of each tradition at its source. Schüssler Fiorenza says that Jesus

> probably understood himself as the prophet and child of Sophia....The earliest Palestinian theological...interpretations of Jesus' life and death understand him as Sophia's messenger and later as Sophia herself.... The earliest Christian theology is Sophialogy.

Once again, Julian is shown to be on solid scriptural ground. As a woman, looking at Scripture in the light of her own experience, Schüssler Fiorenza finds, as did Julian, the female imagery of the wisdom tradition incorporated in the Sophialogy of Christ. "The Sophia-God of Jesus," Schüssler

Fiorenza says, "made possible the invitation of women to the discipleship of equals." Like Goddess-spirituality, Sophialogy empowered early Christian women to see themselves in the divine image, and to act from that strength.

The Motherhood at Work

Julian herself is empowered in the same way by her understanding of the motherhood of God. Early in her life, as she wrote the short text of the *Showings,* before arriving at the motherhood image, Julian describes herself as "a woman, ignorant, weak and frail" (Chapter vi). She takes her first step toward empowerment in her decision to share her vision: "But because I am a woman," she asks, "ought I therefore to believe that I should not tell you of the goodness of God, when I saw at that same time that it is [God's] will that it be known?" She decides to share her vision because it comes from Jesus, "who is everyone's teacher." She does not yet believe that as a woman she should expound her ideas in her own right.

By the time Julian writes the long text, she no longer expresses doubt that as a woman she ought to share her ideas. She refers to herself with continuing humility as "a simple, unlettered creature" (Chapter 2), but there is no longer any apology for being female. For by this time Julian has arrived at an understanding in which God has become mother to us, because "the mother's service is nearest, readiest, and surest: nearest because it is most natural, readiest because it is most loving, and surest because it is truest" (Chapter 60). With the highest understanding of God being motherhood, Julian no longer apologizes for her womanhood, for womanhood has itself become the way in which she resembles Christ.

Just as this imagery empowers women, it also invites men to open themselves to a new understanding of God and of themselves as nurturers. So Thomas Merton praises Sophia in *New Seeds of Contemplation:* "In Sophia, the highest wisdom-principle, all the greatness and majesty of the unknown that is in God and all that is rich and maternal...are united insepa-rably." When both women and men see divinity as female, the fullness of the Spirit shines forth, and we are all enriched in our understanding.

We have seen how Julian's theology answers our needs for centering, spiritual renewal, a positive, experiential theology, and feminine imagery. Yet perhaps her greatest gift to her age and to our own is not these, but her invitation to open our-selves to seeing God as she does. In the last chapter of the long text, Julian says, "this book is begun by God's gift and...grace but it is not yet performed, as I see it." (Chapter 86). Julian says it is when we all join in God's working in prayer, thanking, trusting, and rejoicing that we draw closest to God, because God is the foundation of our beseeching.

What does she mean by this? In Chapter 10 she says, "I saw [God] and I sought [God]...and this is our ordinary undertaking in this life, as I see it." It is in seeking the divine that we find it, because God is the foundation of our longing for the divine.

For Julian, and I think for us, this seeking must begin with-in us, in our own hearts. Starhawk, a peace activist and leader in the feminist spirituality and ecofeminist movements, quotes the traditional Wiccan "Charge of the Goddess": "If that which you seek you find not within yourself, you will never find it without. For behold, I have been with you from the beginning, and I am that which is attained at the end of desire." For Julian, prayer is not only beseeching and seeking, it is beholding as well, and beyond, into oneing with the divine. Ritamary Bradley, in her book *Praying with Julian of Norwich,* writes, "We are, nonetheless, partners with God, in the deed that is being done, in helping form the city which is where God reigns."

If we open ourselves to asking to love God better, as Julian does, and then trust what we see and hear and feel and touch and think as a result, we will begin to form the city within. When we search for precedent and understanding, and then share our insights with others, we participate in what Julian calls "the bliss of our motherhood in Christ." (Chapter 63). It is this that allows us to "begin anew in the joys of...God, which new beginning will last, newly beginning without end" (Chapter 63).

This is the motherhood at work, in which everything is permeated, "in length and in breadth, in height and in depth without end, and it is all one love" (Chapter 59). It is this love, the unconditional love that Julian expresses in divine Motherhood, that is the ultimate meaning of her revelations. In the last chapter of the long text of *Showings,* Julian writes of asking to know the meaning of the revelations. She is answered in "spiritual understanding" that the meaning is love: it is love who reveals it to her, love that is revealed, and love is the purpose for which it is revealed (Chapter 86).

In her overwhelmingly positive anthropology, Julian is convinced that the knowledge we have from our own experience is evidence that we are loved, and comes forth from the source of love which is within us. This is emphasized throughout Chapter 86 of the long text, written after many years of contemplation: "Remain in this, and you will know more of the same. But you will never know different, without end," Julian is told in spirit. In the face of death, cultural change, persecution, and confusion, Julian finds her source in the love that is "without beginning." At the very end of Chapter 86 Julian speaks with one more birthing image: "In this love we have our beginning, and all this we shall see in God without end."

This continual birthing is both God's activity and our own. In time of upheaval, when much around us seems to be changing for the worse, we are called to participate in the spiritual birthgiving of our Mother, who is love. When we open ourselves to the love within, bring forth the light of our inner vision, and then share our insight with one another, we join in this birthgiving. As new insights come forth, we put them to work in the world, "onyd" with the Motherhood. In this way, wisdom renews all things, and through this endless renewing, "all will be well."

Questions for Reflection and Discussion

1. Merton cites Julian's admission that there is no intellectual solution to the problem of evil even as she trusts that "all will be well." What does the phrase "all will be well" mean to you, especially in light of evidence that all is *not* well?

2. Julian ponders the discrepancy between the blame for sin assigned to humanity and the blamelessness God has for us in her vision. Do you feel you are to blame for things you have done which are not good? If you have done unkind things, how do you get back in balance?

3. Why is motherhood imagery universal? What does motherhood mean to you? What does this imagery have to say about the divine? Do you feel that the core symbols of Christianity are inadequate for women? Why or why not?

4. Do you see yourself in Christ? If not, would this change if Christ were seen in female imagery? Do you think a woman can be saved by a male savior? How do you relate to salvation imagery?

5. Does your spirituality reflect your own experience? Are there areas in which it does not ring true with your feelings?

Have you changed your spiritual concepts to match your experience? How did you do this? If you have not made changes, would you like to?

6. How has Julian's motherhood imagery changed your thinking about Christ? About the church? About yourself?

Bibliography

Aelred of Rievaulx. "A Rule of Life for a Recluse" in *Treatises and the Pastoral Prayer.* Kalamazoo, MI: Cistercian Publications, 1971.

Aldredge-Clanton, Jann. *In Search of the Christ-Sophia: An Inclusive Christology for Liberating Christians.* Mystic, CT: Twenty-Third Publications, 1995.

Allchin, A. M. "Julian of Norwich and the Continuity of Tradition." *Julian: Woman of Our Day.* Robert Llewelyn, ed. Mystic, CT: Twenty-Third Publications, 1987.

Bolton, Brenda M. "Mulieres Sanctae." *Women in Medieval Society.* Susan Mosher Stuard, ed. Philadephia: University of Pennsylvania Press, 1976.

Bolton, Brenda M. "Vitae Matrum: A Further Aspect of the Frauenfrage." *Medieval Women.* Derek Baker, ed. (Studies in Church History: Subsidia I). Cambridge, MA: Blackwell Publications, 1978.

Bradley, Ritamary. "Julian on Prayer." *Peaceweavers.* Lillian Thomas Shank and John A. Nichols, eds. (Cistercian Studies Series 72). Kalamazoo, MI: Cistercian Publications, 1987.

Bradley, Ritamary. *Julian's Way: A Practical Commentary on Julian of Norwich.* San Francisco: Harper San Francisco, 1992.

Bradley, Ritamary. "The Motherhood Theme in Julian of Norwich." *Fourteenth Century English Mystics Newsletter* 2, no. 4 (1976).

Bradley, Ritamary. "Patristic Background of the Motherhood Similitude in Julian of Norwich." *Christian Scholar's Review* 8 (1978).

Bynum, Caroline Walker. *Holy Feast and Holy Fast: The Religious Significance of Food to Medieval Women.* Berkeley: University of California Press, 1987.

Bynum, Caroline Walker. *Jesus as Mother: Studies in the Spirituality of the High Middle Ages.* Berkeley: University of California Press, 1982.

Carlton, Lee. Personal interview, August 2, 1994.

Colledge, Edmund and James Walsh, trans. *A Book of Showings to the Anchoress Julian of Norwich,* 2 volumes (Studies and Texts 35). Toronto: Pontifical Institute of Medieval Studies, 1978.

Colledge, Edmund and James Walsh, trans. *Julian of Norwich: Showings* (The Classics of Western Spirituality Series). Mahwah, NJ: Paulist Press, 1978.

Conn, Joann Wolski. "Women's Spirituality: Restriction and Reconstruction." *Women's Spirituality: Resources for Christian Development.* Joann Wolski Conn, ed. Mahwah, NJ: Paulist Press, 1986.

Crampton, Georgia Ronan, ed. *The Shewings of Julian of Norwich.* TEAMS-Medieval Institute Publications. Kalamazoo, MI: Western Michigan University Press, 1994.

Cummings, Charles. "The Motherhood of God According to Julian of Norwich." *Peaceweavers.* Lillian Thomas Shank and John A. Nichols, eds. (Cistercian Studies Series 72). Kalamazoo, MI: Cistercian Publications, 1987.

Denley, Peter. "The Mediterranean in the Age of the Renaissance, 1200-1500." *The Oxford Illustrated History of Medieval Europe.* George Holmes, ed. New York: Oxford University Press, 1988.

Fitzmyer, Joseph A. *The Gospel According to Luke (I-IX)* (The Anchor Bible Series 28). New York: Doubleday, 1981.

Gearhart, Sally. "The Lesbian and God-the-Father." *Radical Religion* 1, no. 2 (1974); reprinted in *WomanSpirit* 1, no. 1 (1974).

Gimbutas, Marija. *The Language of the Goddess: Unearthing the Hidden Symbols of Western Civilization.* San Francisco: Harper SF, 1989.

Gottfried, Robert S. *The Black Death: Natural and Human Disaster in Medieval Europe.* New York: The Free Press, 1983.

Greer, Rowan A., trans. *Origen: Selected Writings* (The Classics of Western Spirituality Series). Mahwah, NJ: Paulist Press, 1979.

Hebblethwaite, Margaret. *Motherhood and God.* London: Chapman-Cassell, 1984.

Heimmel, Jennifer P. *"God is Our Mother": Julian of Norwich and the Medieval Image of Christian Feminine Divinity* (Elizabethan & Renaissance Studies 92:5). Salzburg: University of Salzburg Press, 1982.

Jantzen, Grace M. *Julian of Norwich: Mystic and Theologian.* Mahwah, NJ: Paulist Press, 1988.

Johnson, Lynn Staley. "The Trope of the Scribe and the Question of Literary Authority in the Works of Julian of Norwich and Margery Kempe." *Speculum* 66, no. 4 (1991).

Labarge, Margaret Wade. *A Small Sound of the Trumpet: Women in Medieval Life.* Boston: Beacon Press, 1986.

Leclercq, Jean. "Solitude and Solidarity: Medieval Women Recluses." *Peaceweavers.* Lillian Thomas Shank and John A. Nichols, eds. (Cistercian Studies Series 72). Kalamazoo, MI: Cistercian Publications, 1987.

Lentz, Robert. "Julian of Norwich." Burlington, VT: Bridge Building Images, 1995.

Lerner, Robert E. "The Black Death and Western European Eschatological Mentalities." *The Black Death: The Impact of the Fourteenth-Century Plague.* Daniel Williman, ed. (Medieval & Renaissance Texts & Studies 13). Binghamton, NY: Center for Medieval & Early Renaissance Studies, 1982.

Manning, Bernard L. "England: Edward III and Richard II." *Decline of the Empire and Papacy* (The Cambridge Medieval History 7). New York: Cambridge University Press, 1932.

McLean, Michael. Introduction. *Julian: Woman of Our Day.* Robert Llewelyn, ed. Mystic, CT: Twenty-Third Publications, 1987.

Meech, Sanford Brown and Hope Emily Allen, eds. *The Book of Margery Kempe.* (Early English Text Society Series) New York: Oxford University Press, 1940.

Merton, Thomas. *Conjectures of a Guilty Bystander.* New York: Doubleday, 1966.

Merton, Thomas. *Mystics and Zen Masters.* New York: Delta-Dell, 1967.

Merton, Thomas. *New Seeds of Contemplation.* New York: New Directions, 1961.

Merton, Thomas. *Seeds of Destruction.* New York: Farrar, Straus & Giroux, 1964.

Mott, Michael. *The Seven Mountains of Thomas Merton.* Boston: Houghton Mifflin, 1984.

Mountaingrove, Jean. "Explorations in the Grove." *WomanSpirit* 1, no. 1 (1974).

Mountaingrove, Ruth. "A Gift to Myself: A Menstrual Experiment." *WomanSpirit* 1, no. 2 (1974).

Nuth, Joan M. *Wisdom's Daughter: The Theology of Julian of Norwich.* New York: The Crossroad Publishing Co., 1991.

Pezzini, Domenico. "The Theme of the Passion in Richard Rolle and Julian of Norwich." *Religion in the Poetry and Drama of the Late Middle Ages.* Piero Boitani and Anna Torti, ed. Rochester, NY: Brewer-Boydell, 1990.

Previte-Orton, C. W. *The Twelfth Century to the Renaissance.* (The Shorter Cambridge Medieval History 2). New York: Cambridge University Press, 1966.

Reynolds, Anna Maria. "Woman of Hope." *Julian: Woman of Our Day.* Robert Llewelyn, ed. Mystic, CT: Twenty-Third Publications, 1987.

Rosof, Patricia J. F. "The Anchoress in the Twelfth and Thirteenth Centuries." *Peaceweavers.* Lillian Thomas Shank and John A. Nichols, eds. (Cistercian Studies Series 72). Kalamazoo, MI: Cistercian Publications, 1987.

Savage, Anne and Nicholas Watson, trans. "Ancrene Wisse." *Anchoritic Spirituality: Ancrene Wisse and Associated Works* (Classics of Western Spiritulaity Series). Mahwah, NJ: Paulist Press, 1991.

Schüssler Fiorenza, Elisabeth. "The Sophia-God of Jesus and the Discipleship of Women." *Women's Spirituality: Resources for Christian Development.* Joann Wolski Conn, ed. Mahwah, NJ: Paulist Press, 1986.

Stramara, Daniel F. "El Shaddai: A Feminine Aspect of God." *The Pecos Benedictine,* Leaflet 28.

Starhawk. *The Spiral Dance: A Rebirth of the Ancient Religion of the Great Goddess.* 10th anniversary edition. New York: HarperCollins, 1989.

Swanson, John. "Guide for the Inexpert Mystic." *Julian: Woman of Our Day.* Robert Llewelyn, ed. Mystic, CT: Twenty-Third Publications, 1987.

Tuchman, Barbara W. *A Distant Mirror: The Calamitous 14th Century*. New York: Knopf, 1978.

Twigg, Graham. *The Black Death: A Biological Reappraisal*. London: Batsford, 1984.

Uitz, Erika. *Die Frau in der mittelalterlichen Stadt*. 1988. Reprinted as *The Legend of Good Women: Medieval Women in Towns and Cities*. Mt. Kisco, NY: Moyer Bell, 1990.

Villaro, Albert. "The Reaction of the Citizens of La Seu d'Urgell to the Black Death." Mortimer Bear, trans. *Concilium*, Volume 3, 1993.

Ward, Benedicta, trans. *The Prayers and Meditations of St. Anselm*. New York: Penguin Books, 1973.

Warren, Ann K. *Anchorites and their Patrons in Medieval England*. Berkeley: University of California Press, 1985.

Warren, Ann K. "The Nun as Anchoress: England 1100-1500." *Distant Echoes*. John A. Nichols and Lillian Thomas Shank, eds. (Cistercian Studies Series 71). Kalamazoo, MI: Cistercian Publications, 1984.

"Why WomanSpirit?" *WomanSpirit* 1, no. 1, 1974.

Wolters, Clifton, trans. *Julian of Norwich: Revelations of Divine Love*. New York: Penguin Books, 1966.